For my father,
who was once mistaken
for an analyst.

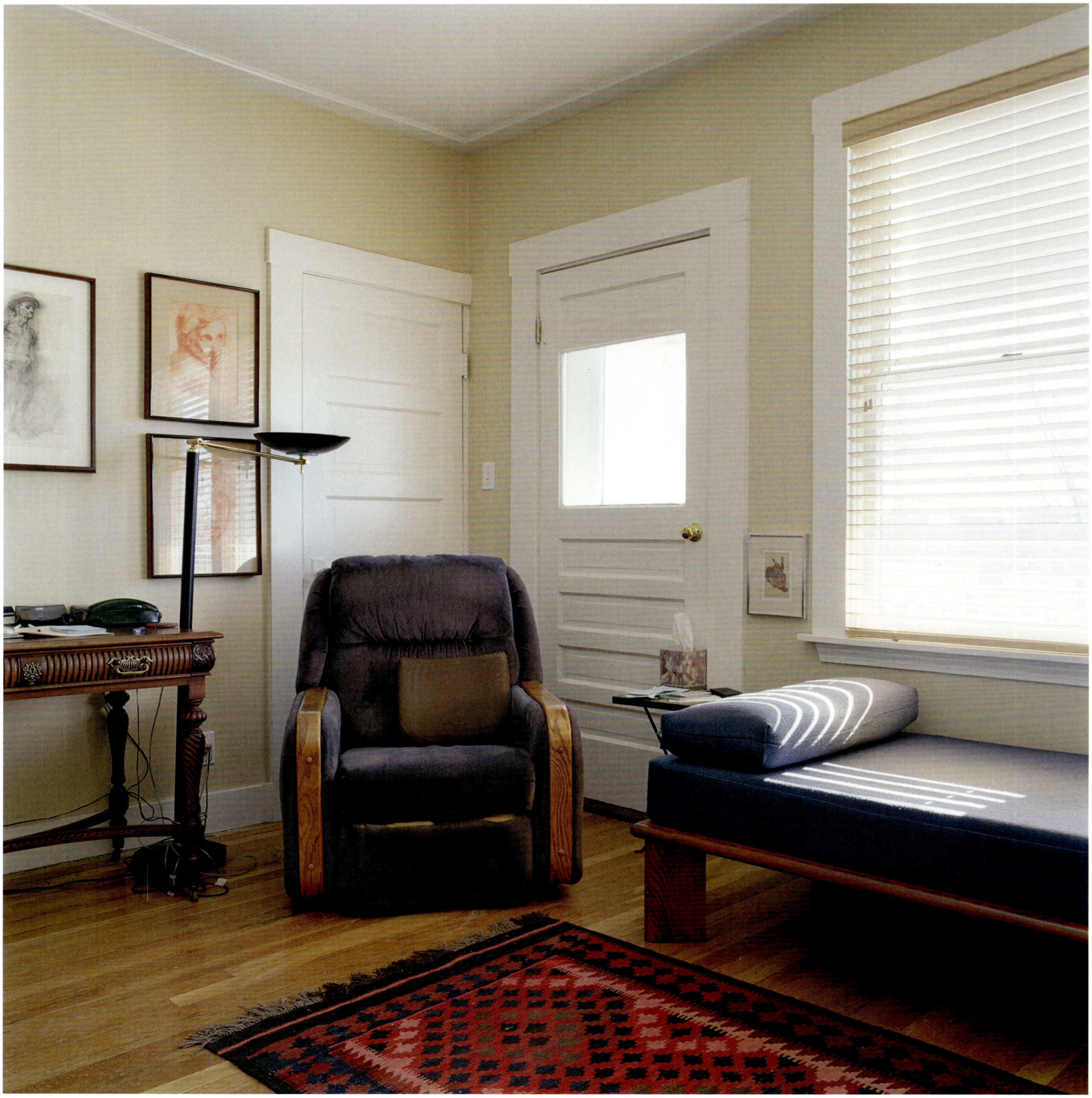

ANALYSIS

Shellburne Thurber

KEHRER

PSYCHOANALYTIC INTERIORS

Lia Gangitano

Returning to Shellburne Thurber's psychoanalytic interiors, as I have many times in the more than twenty years since she first began making them, it is tempting to locate my implicit sense of the photographs as "structures for feeling" through artist and theorist Jill H. Casid's queer theory of "pyrography." In her essay "Pyrographies: Photography and the good death," a close reading of Hervé Guibert's photo-novel *Suzanne and Louise* through the writings of his friends (namely, Michel Foucault's "The Social Triumph of the Sexual Will" and Roland Barthes's *Camera Lucida* and *Mourning Diary*), Casid correlates photography's unstable material qualities with the medium's inextricable associations to mourning and death. In it, Casid establishes photography "as a practice of making volatile structures for feeling... not just for mourning the losses that have actually happened but spaces in which one might begin to imagine and transact with care the losses and the letting go yet to come."[1]

In discussing death's rehearsals as photographically enacted by Guibert (both alone and together with his aunts), or wished-for in a proposition to Barthes (to photograph him with his dying mother), Casid also speaks about love, mirrors, re-sequenced time, the untimely, Guibert's photography as a "séance to the future,"[2] and impossible photographs that can't or shouldn't be made. Guibert's 1980 text *Suzanne and Louise* opens with a handwritten title that reads: "A simulacra." It contains black and white photographs of Guibert's elderly aunts performing deathbeds in their home as well as a letter from Hervé to Suzanne that includes the line, "And when you feel yourself about to die, call me..." Published in the same year as *Camera Lucida*, Casid notes: "It is, of course, well known that *Camera Lucida* was Barthes's last book; he died only two months after its French publication. It is also well known that this book on photography is organized around a central and quite specific absence: a photograph of his deceased mother that presents her as a little girl in a greenhouse. He describes it and gives it a name (the 'Winter Garden Photograph'), but refuses to reproduce it: "I cannot reproduce the 'Winter Garden Photograph.' It exists only for me."[3] By unwriting past tense entanglements of loved ones and their pyres, and considering the future perfect "what-will-have-been," Casid establishes "what it means to use photography as a performative rehearsal for the catastrophe that has already happened,"[4] not unlike the process of psychoanalysis itself. In this citation, Casid refers to Barthes' *Mourning Diary*, where he draws from psychoanalyst Donald Winnicott's final paper, "Fear of breakdown," posthumously published in the *International Review of Psycho-Analysis* in 1974. With this contextual background, Thurber's analytic interiors perceive the complex dramaturgies of rehearsal that have occurred in these empty rooms.

While the *subject* of psychoanalysis has appeared in the work of many contemporary artists, particularly through the citation of psychoanalytic theory, Thurber takes another route in arriving at one of her most significant bodies of work—a series of square format chromogenic prints depicting the unoccupied office spaces of psychoanalysts. Initiated in 1998 in Buenos Aires, the project continued through a Bunting Fellowship (Radcliffe Institute for Advanced Study, Harvard University) in 1999–2000, enabling her to pursue the project in the Boston area. Unlike art practices that seek to demonstrate theoretical premises, Thurber's work instead elaborates upon a long photographic history, fusing particular formal concerns with an interest in people: their varying abilities to communicate, and the ways in which the constructed environment (homes, motels, offices) can articulate, by containing, the complexities of the lives that pass through them. The issues most clearly raised by her psychoanalytic interiors and the ideas they evoke—absence, emptiness, the unconscious, the unstable boundaries between self and other—are also subjects of Thurber's work as a whole.

Exhibition projects such as *Boston School* (1995, The ICA, Boston), placed Thurber's work alongside a constellation of peers who, in the mid-seventies, broke with documentary traditions by turning the camera's focus inward. Her investment in the photographic medium continues to reside in its ability to address often claustrophobic familial, intimate, and interpersonal relationships. The quirky intimacy of the psychoanalytic interiors reveals yet another aspect of Thurber's long-standing interest in "holding environments," and the emotionality of space. The fact that people occupy much of Thurber's early work serves to underscore the issue of absence that characterizes the vast majority of her subsequent work. Portraiture and the self-portrait remain a central focus, whether she chooses to photograph a landscape, a house, a room, or a chair. The social character of Thurber's populated early work, however autobiographical, also addresses class anxiety in general—the external realities that separate people, the desire to break away from proscribed social groupings, and the awkward trappings of domestic space—the space that exists between people.

Perhaps the transient spaces of empty motel interiors, photographed in the late seventies, mark the beginning of Thurber's ongoing effort to more fully describe the interior lives of people. In this series, familiar details of generic or institutional décor are emphasized through attention to their rich surfaces. The spaces are often made enigmatic by the presence of reflections—the doubling of the room in a mirror, the space of the television screen, and so many electrical cords. In their strangeness, these images also reveal familiarity—the uncanny sense of looking toward an unstable, mirroric interiority. In Thurber's work, anxieties associated with the latent eccentricities of presumably rational, calculated spaces are depicted as fraught with emotionality and charged with the traces of their absent inhabitants. Her photographs seek to render even an ordinary room or landscape an interior, and the absence of literal human subjects cause a slippage in the continuous displacement of meaning onto seemingly prosaic details. By photographing intensely intimate yet "public," spaces such as motels or offices, Thurber invokes the unique interstices of public and private that these spaces represent, pointing to their layered internal significance.

In the case of the psychoanalytic interiors, Thurber's photographs destabilize pre-conceived perceptions of a "neutral" psychoanalytic office (as impartial projection space for the imaginary or unconscious) by divulging idiosyncrasy amidst methodological order. The photographs elaborate a poetics of repression and displacement, insinuating a disturbance in the presumably impassive organization of space (which almost always includes a well-placed box of tissues). They refer to places, however proscribed, that serve a function of transitory connectedness, holding intimate meaning for many that leave their impressions. Within the relative uniformity of the arrangements and types of furniture, these interiors represent an assertion of complicated affinities, indicating places that refuse to belie their particular, and increasingly outmoded, brands of intimacy. Thurber's project does not seek to document or imitate a set pattern, but instead comments on a cultural moment of growing detachment that would render such places obsolete.

Psychoanalyst and literary theorist Julia Kristeva speaks generally of lost Things: "Naming suffering, exalting it, dissecting it into its smallest components—that is doubtless a way to curb mourning. To revel in it at times, but also to go beyond it, moving on to another form, not so scorching, more and more perfunctory... Nevertheless, art seems to point to a few devices that bypass complacency and, without simply turning mourning into mania, secure for the artist [...] a sublimatory hold over the lost Thing."[5] As Thurber remarks in her interview with Jess T. Dugan, a connectedness seems to exist between the psychoanalytic work and her earliest interior photographs, first taken in her grandmother's house in Indiana in the '70s while seeking clues about her deceased mother. As she further describes in this interview, the rays of light in her aunt's empty house coming through the windows evoke her spirit more fully than the weighed down presence of her belongings. Casid goes further to define photography's more specific, perhaps actually scorching aim: "To understand photography as a way of representing what has died as wanting to be alive recasts the spectator's wish for the return of the loved and lost or for the loved and lost to wish to return as the 'want' of the photograph. It is also to reconceive the spectator's encounter with the photograph as not a means of getting close to death but rather [...] holding the cord of the fantasy of a returned love one never has to lose."[6]

1 —— Jill H. Casid, "Pyrographies: Photography and the Good Death," *Women & Performance: a journal of feminist theory 22*, no. 1 (2012): 109–131.
2 —— Casid, 117.
3 —— Casid, citing Roland Barthes, *Camera Lucida*, 110.
4 —— Casid, citing Roland Barthes, *Mourning Diary*, 112.
5 —— Julia Kristeva, "Beauty: The Depressive's Other Realm," in *Black Sun: Depression and Melancholia*, (New York: Columbia University Press, 1989), 97.
6 —— Casid, 111.

Buenos Aires
Analyst's desk with flowers and hand-shaped paperweight, 1999

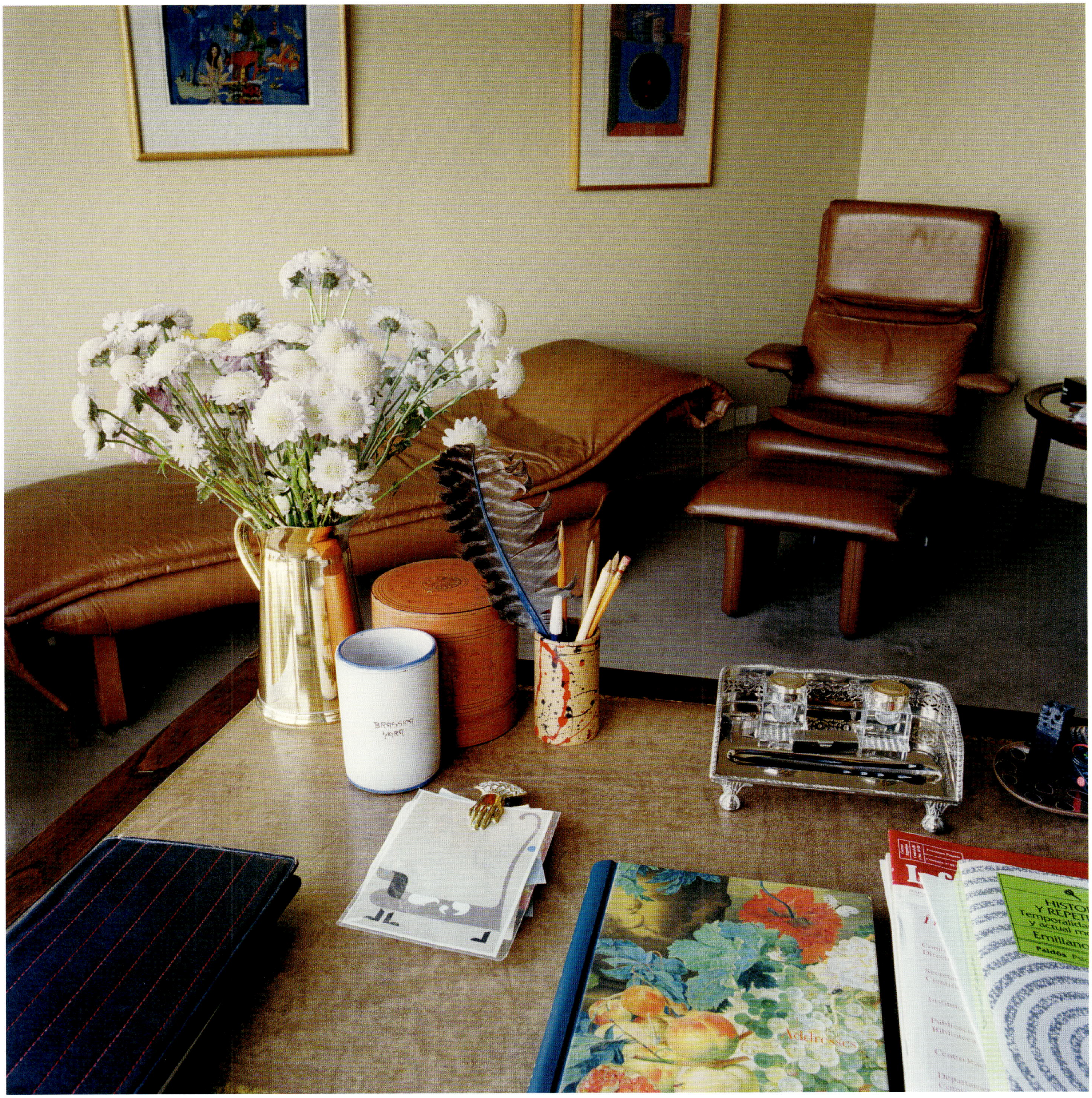
Addresses

Brookline, MA
Hospital office with blue fabric couch, 2000

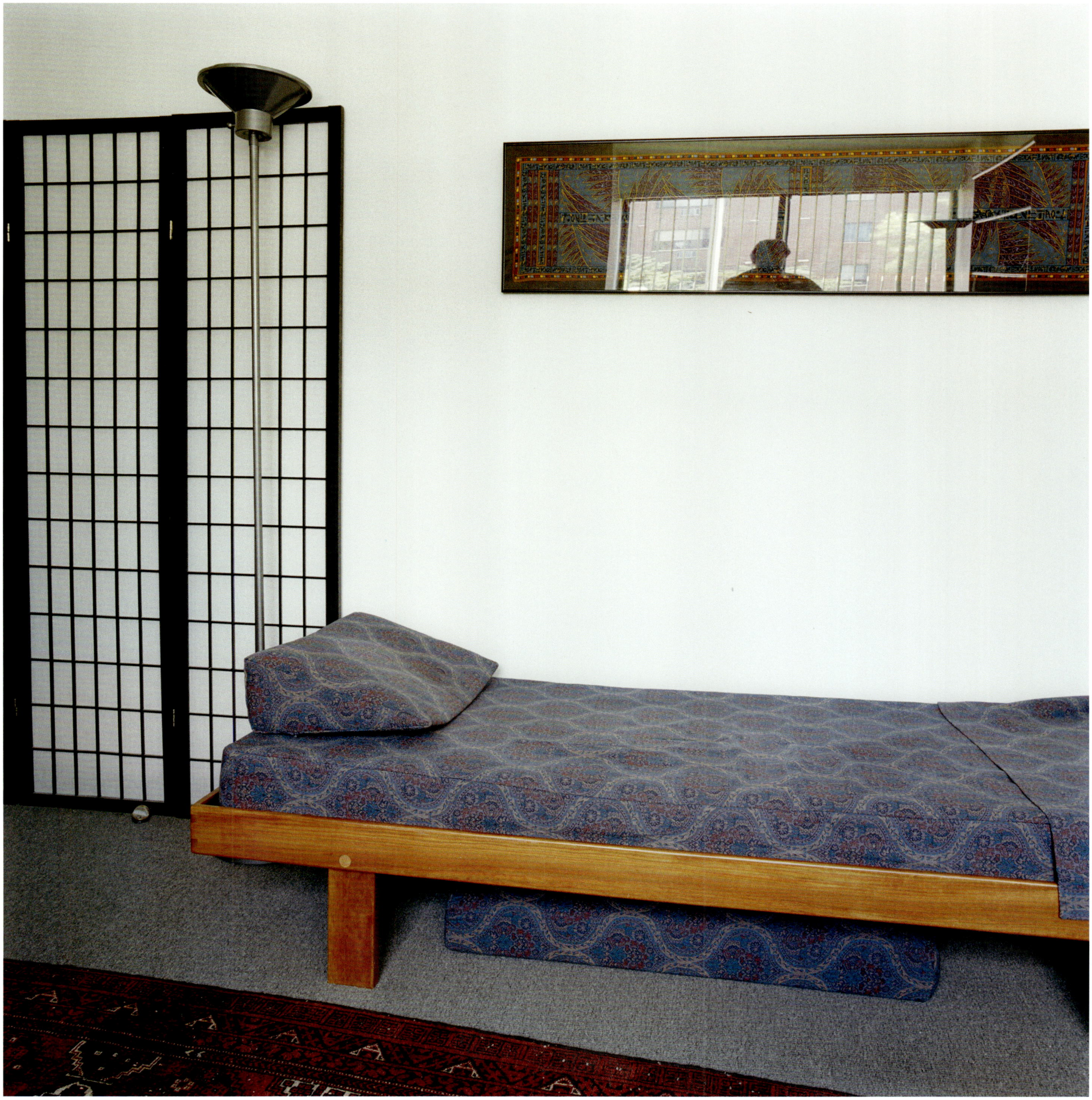

Stockbridge, MA
Analyst's desk with black leather chair and wall diplomas, 2000

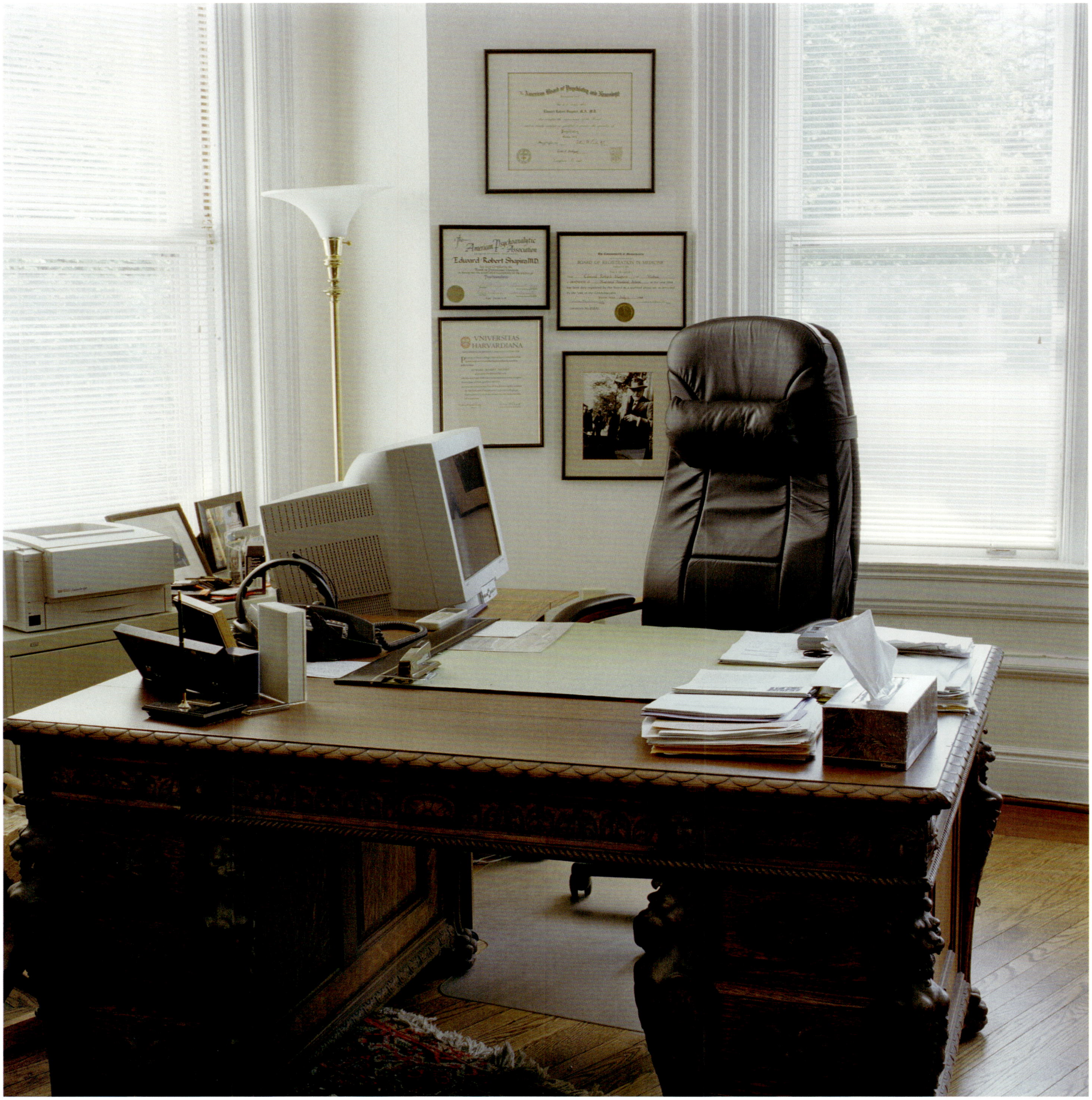
The American Psychoanalytic Association
Edward Robert Shapiro M.D.
VNIVERSITAS HARVARDIANA

Buenos Aires
Office with peach-colored wall, 1999

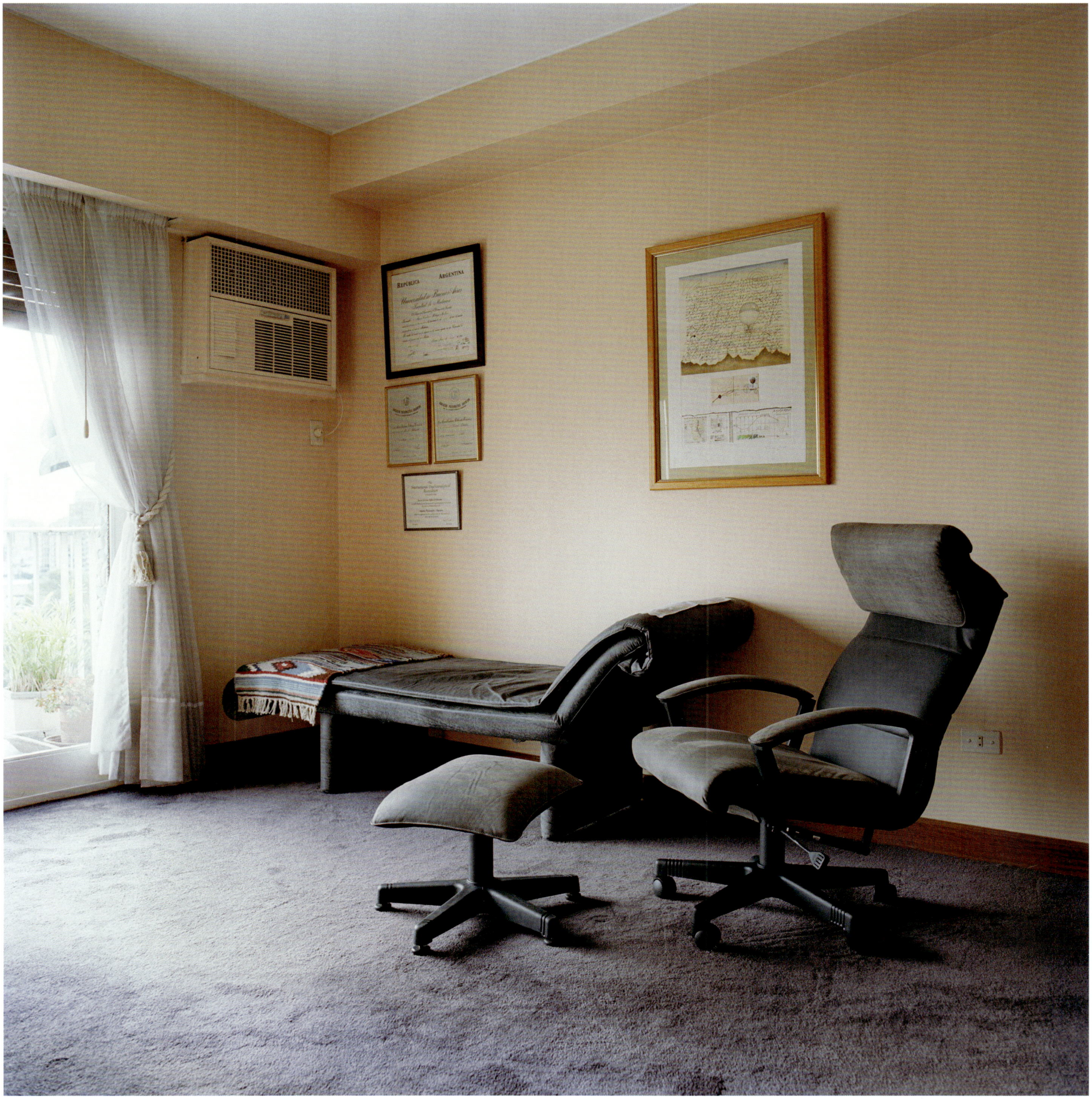
REPUBLICA ARGENTINA

Buenos Aires
Green plush analyst's chair with embroidered antimacassar, 1999

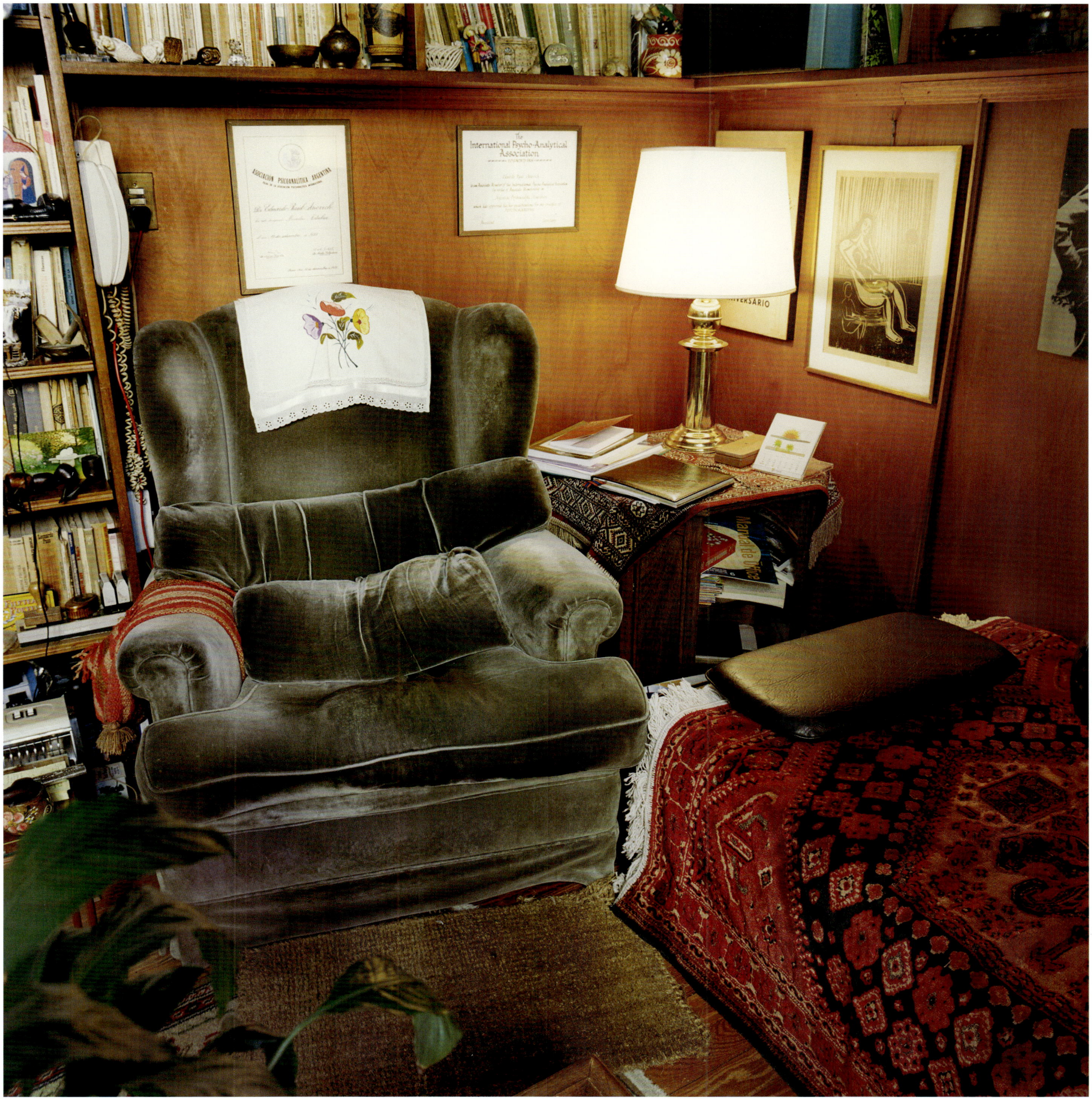
The International Psycho-Analytical Association

Lexington, MA
Office with two plush orange patient's chairs, 2000

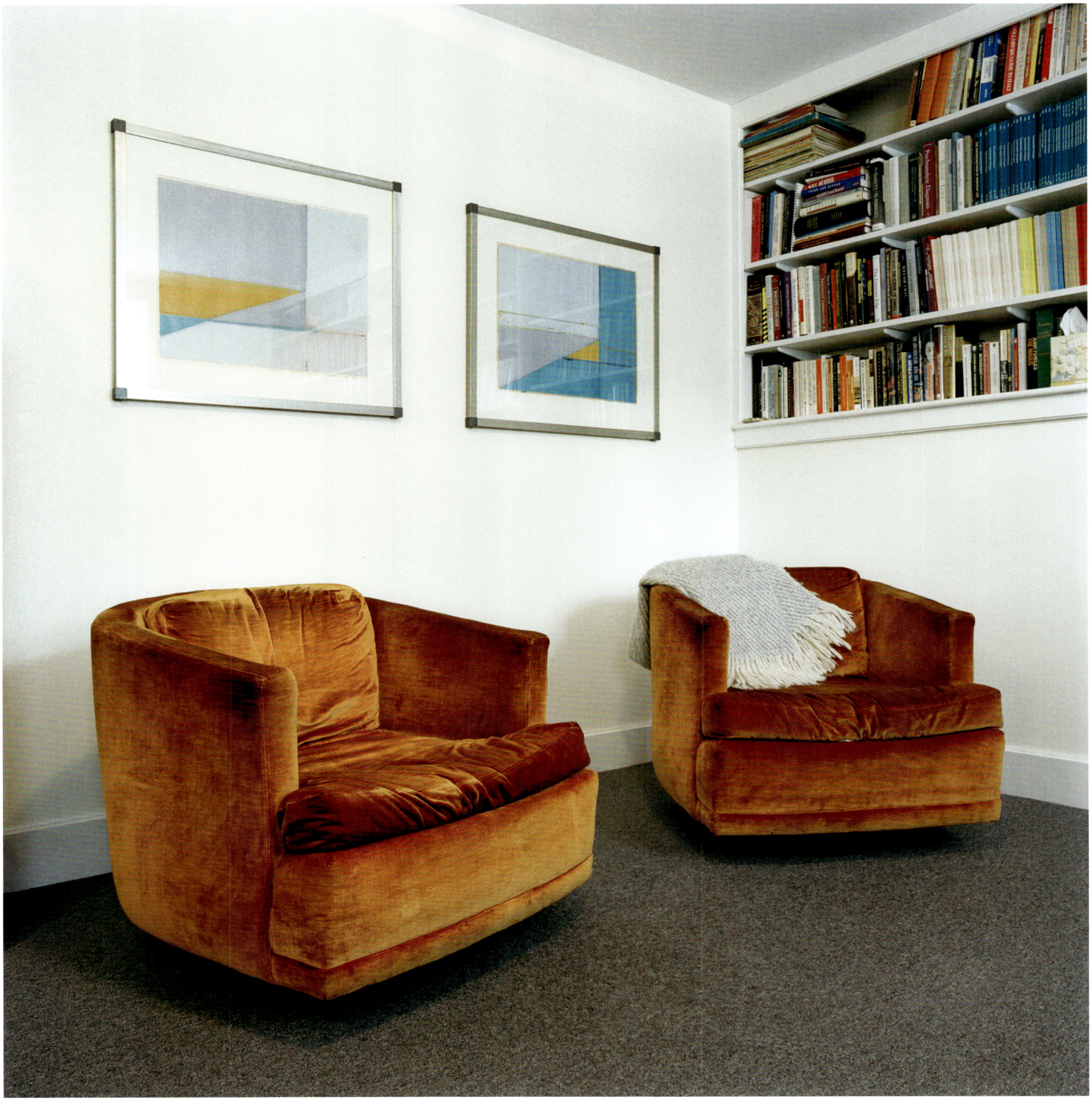

Cambridge, MA
Basement office with pink analyst's chair and couch, 2000

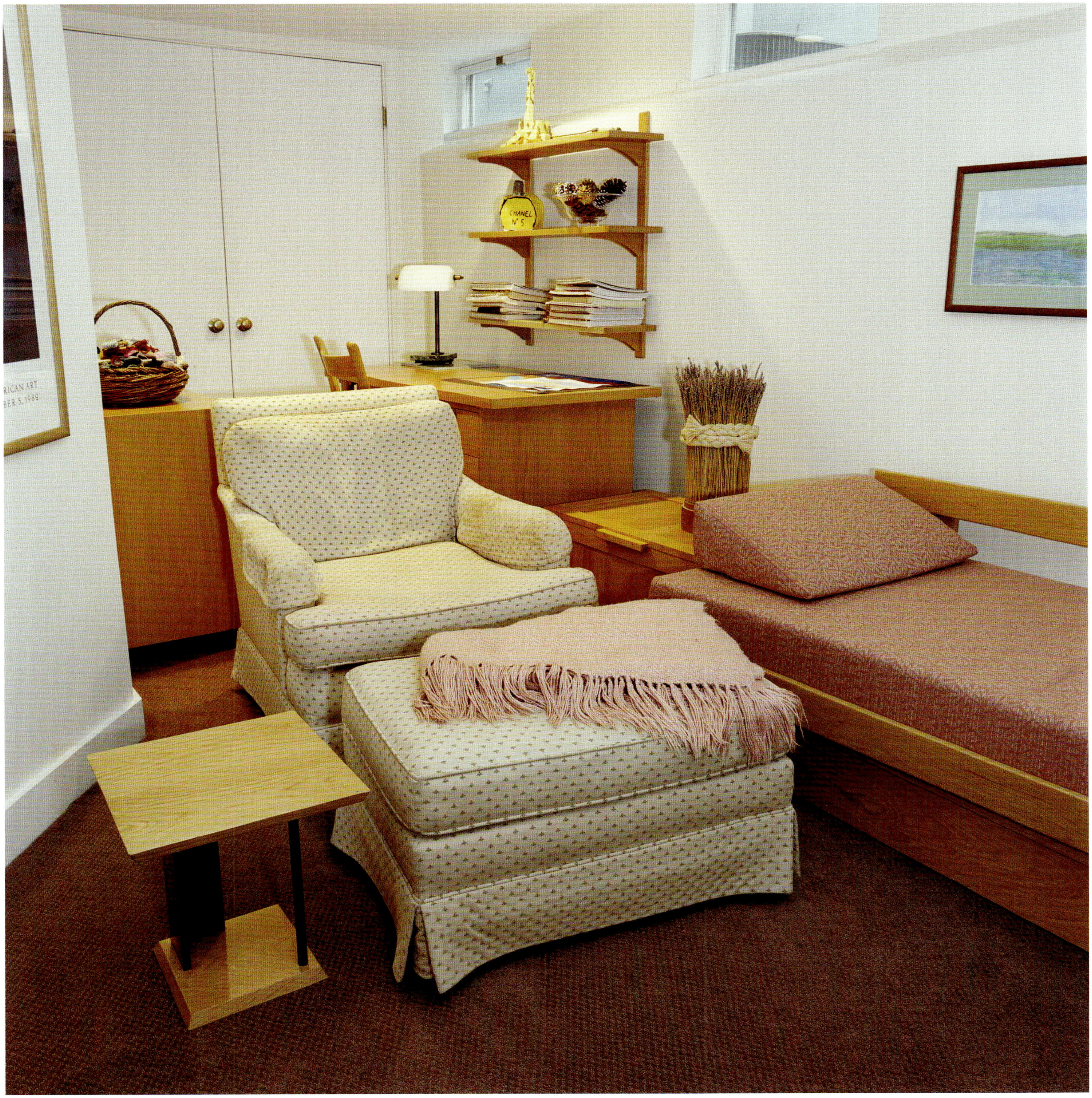
CHANEL

Cambridge, MA
Basement office with easel and small fabric wall hanging, 2000

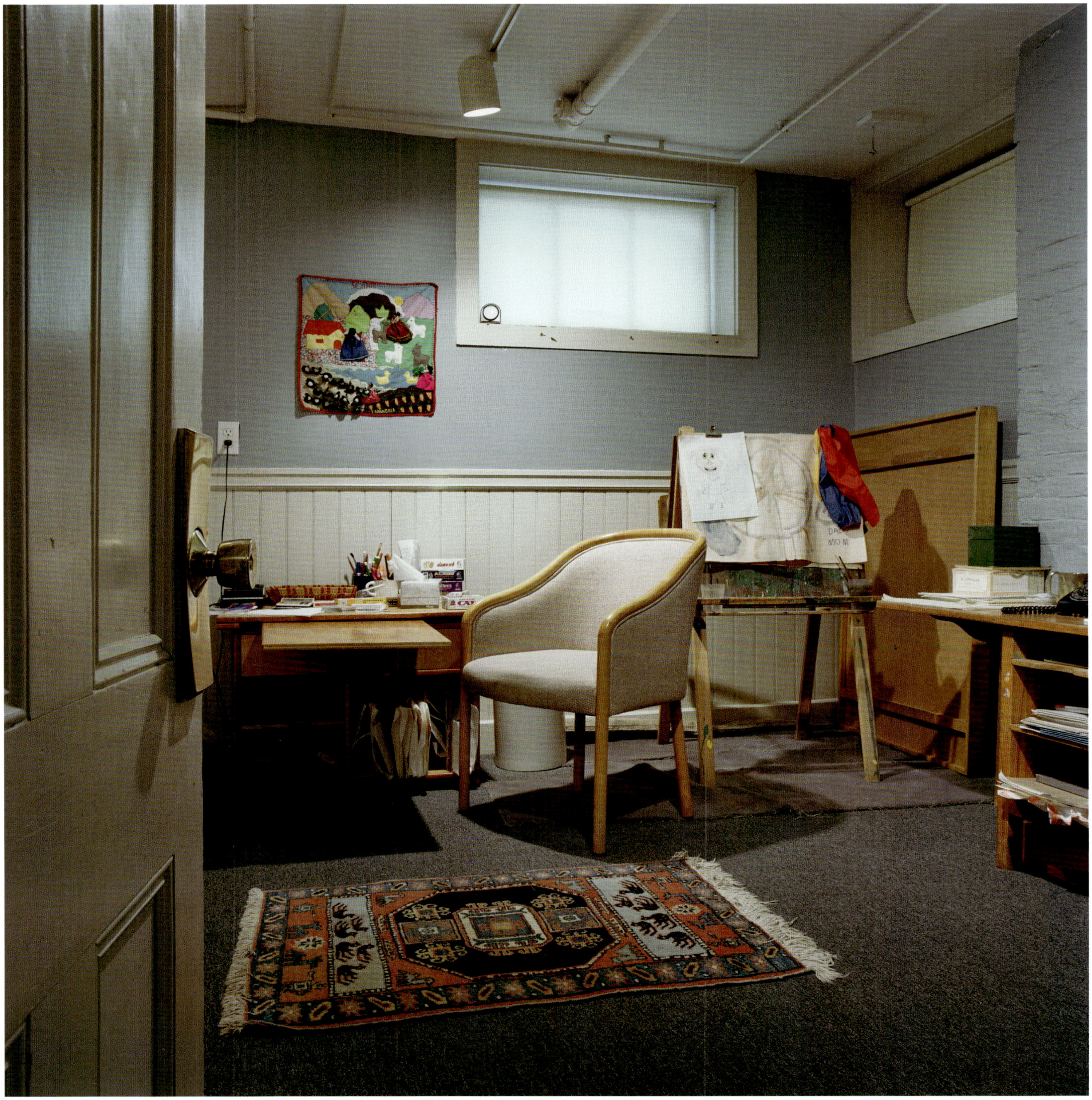

Buenos Aires
Office with floor-to-ceiling window and sheer curtains, 1999

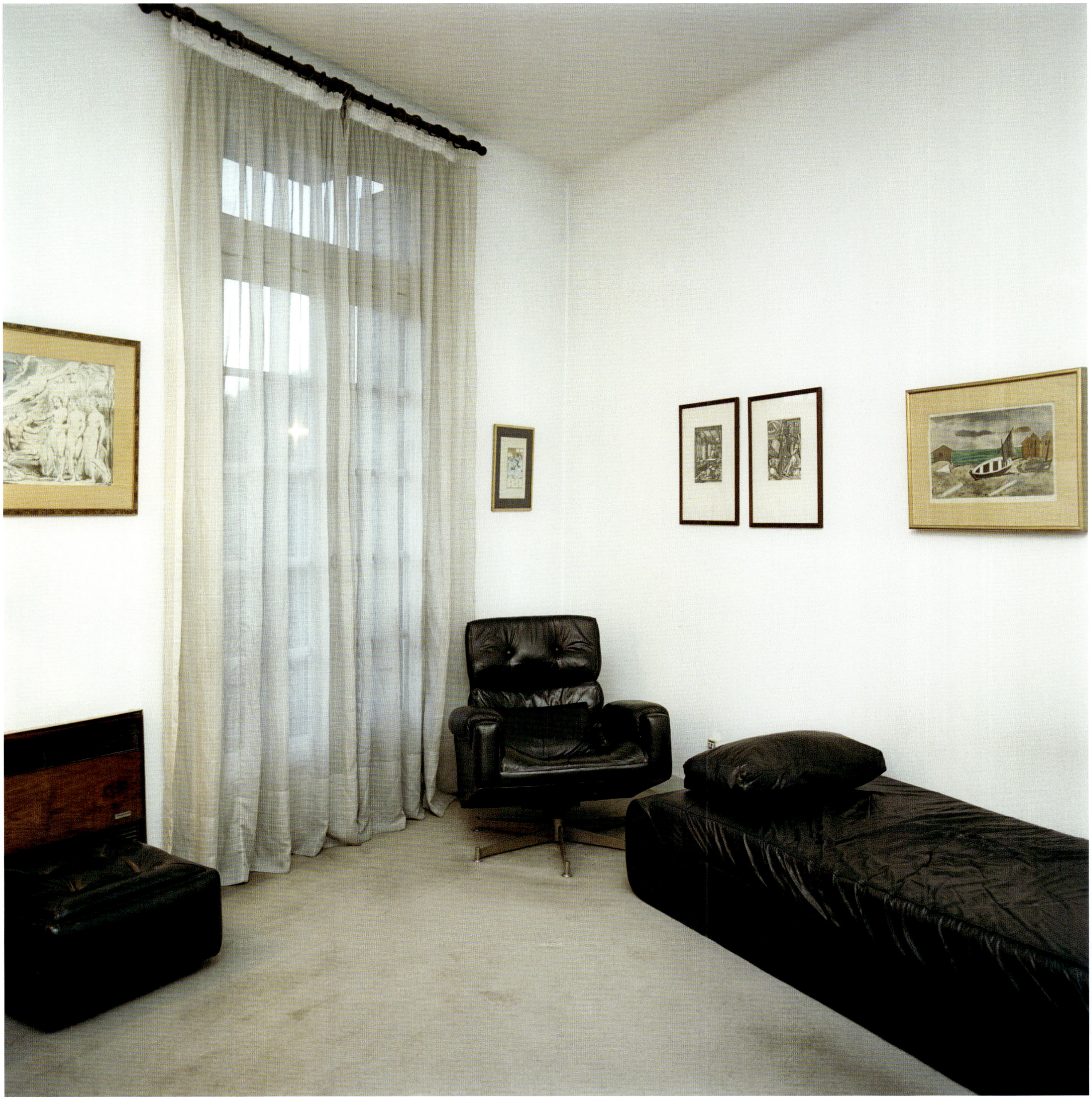

Buenos Aires
Waiting room with red wall and two chairs, 1999

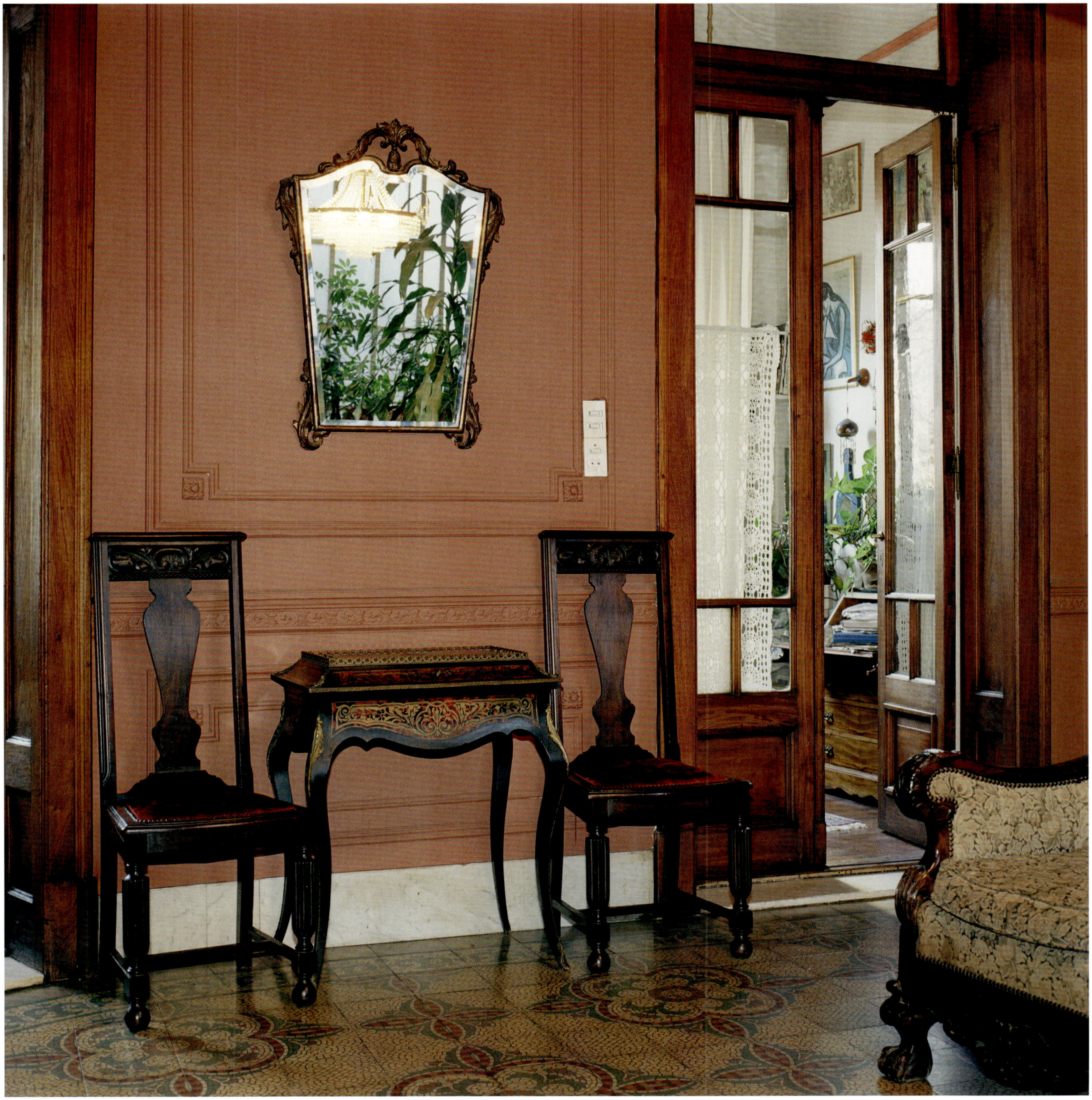

Brookline, MA
Porch office with antique couch and clown print, 2000

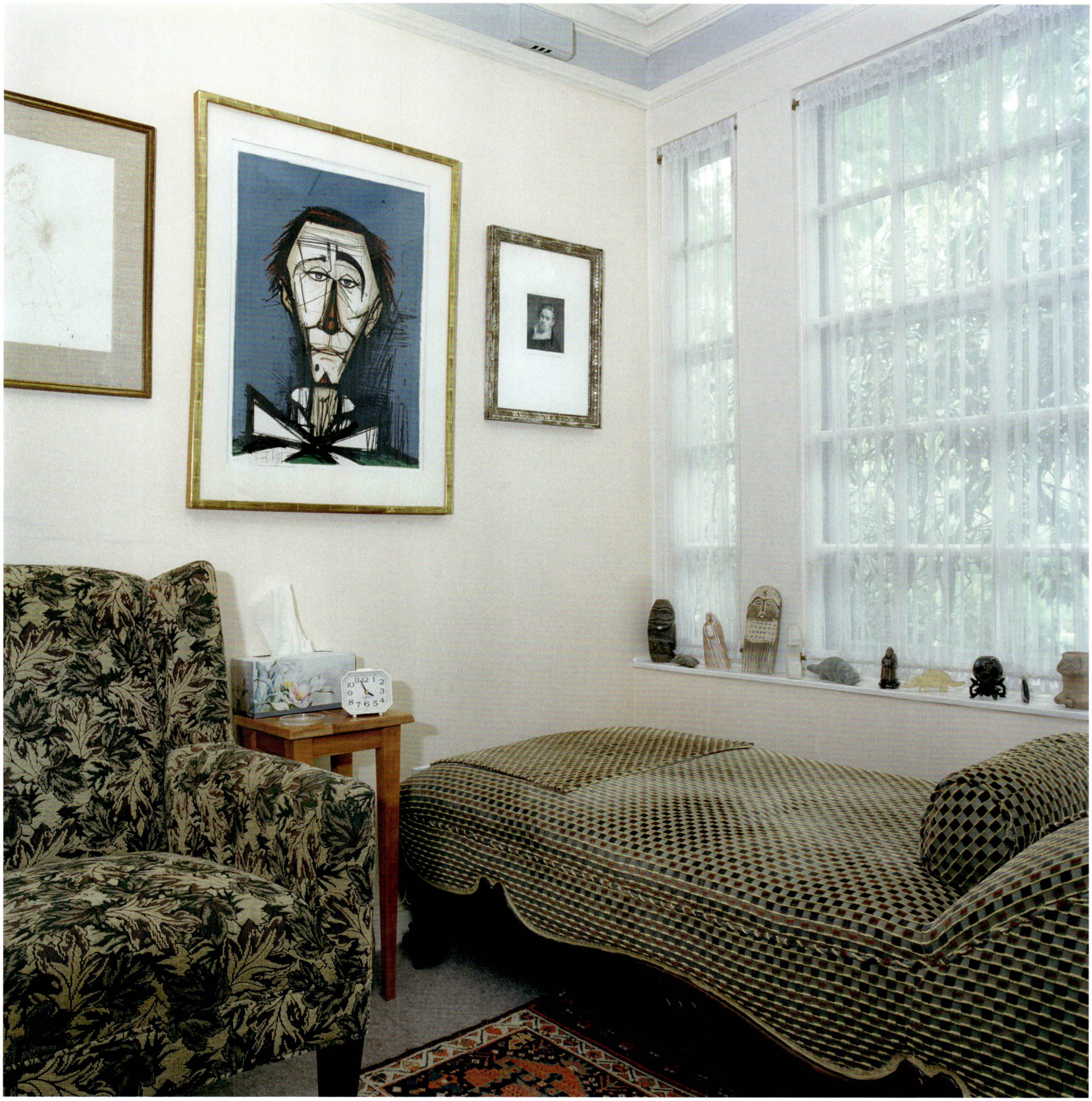

Chestnut Hill, MA
Analyst's office with soft green couch and dollhouse, 2000

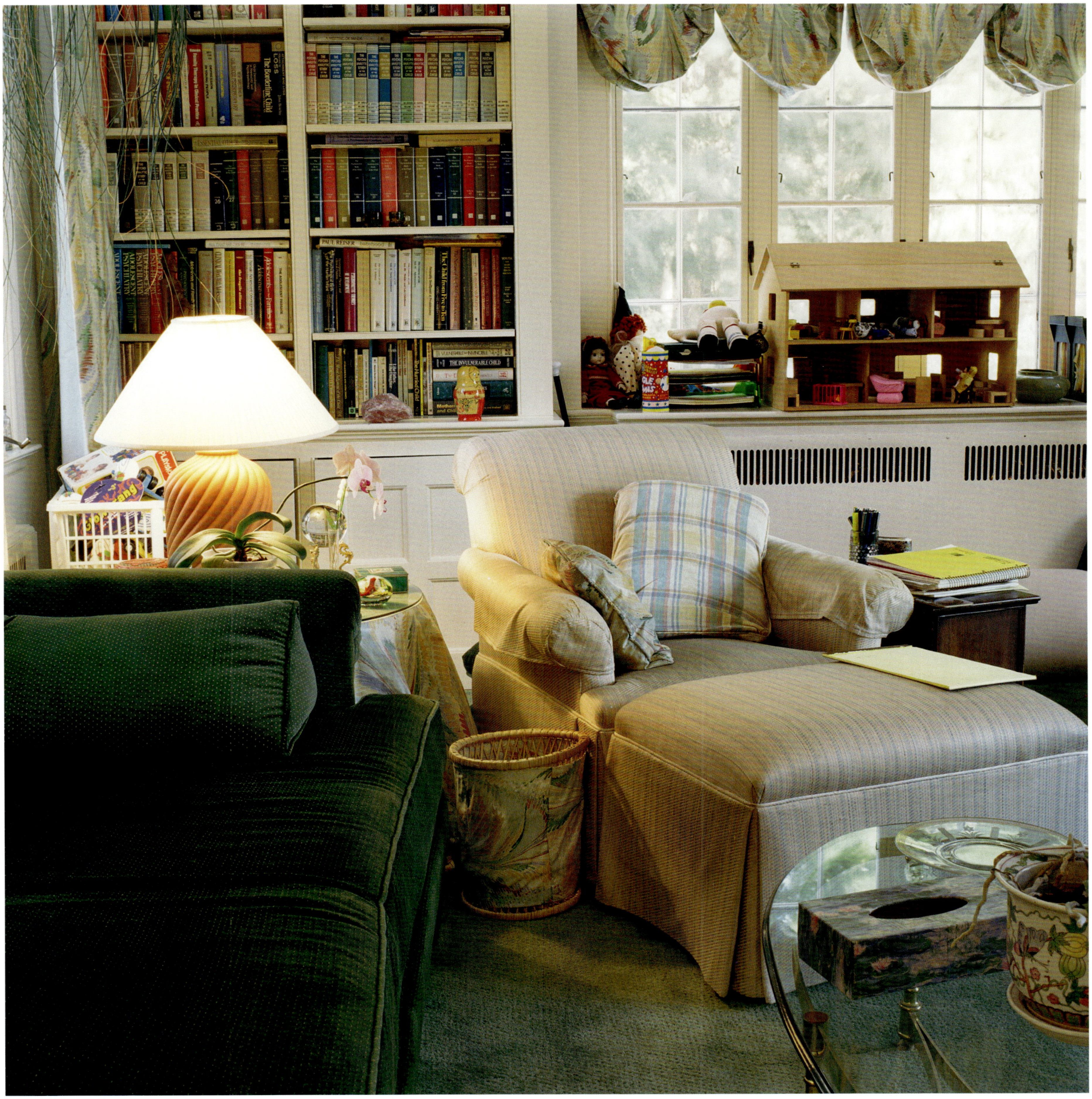
PAUL REISER
THE INVULNERABLE CHILD

Lexington, MA
Analyst's office with flowered tissue box and pastel painting, 2000

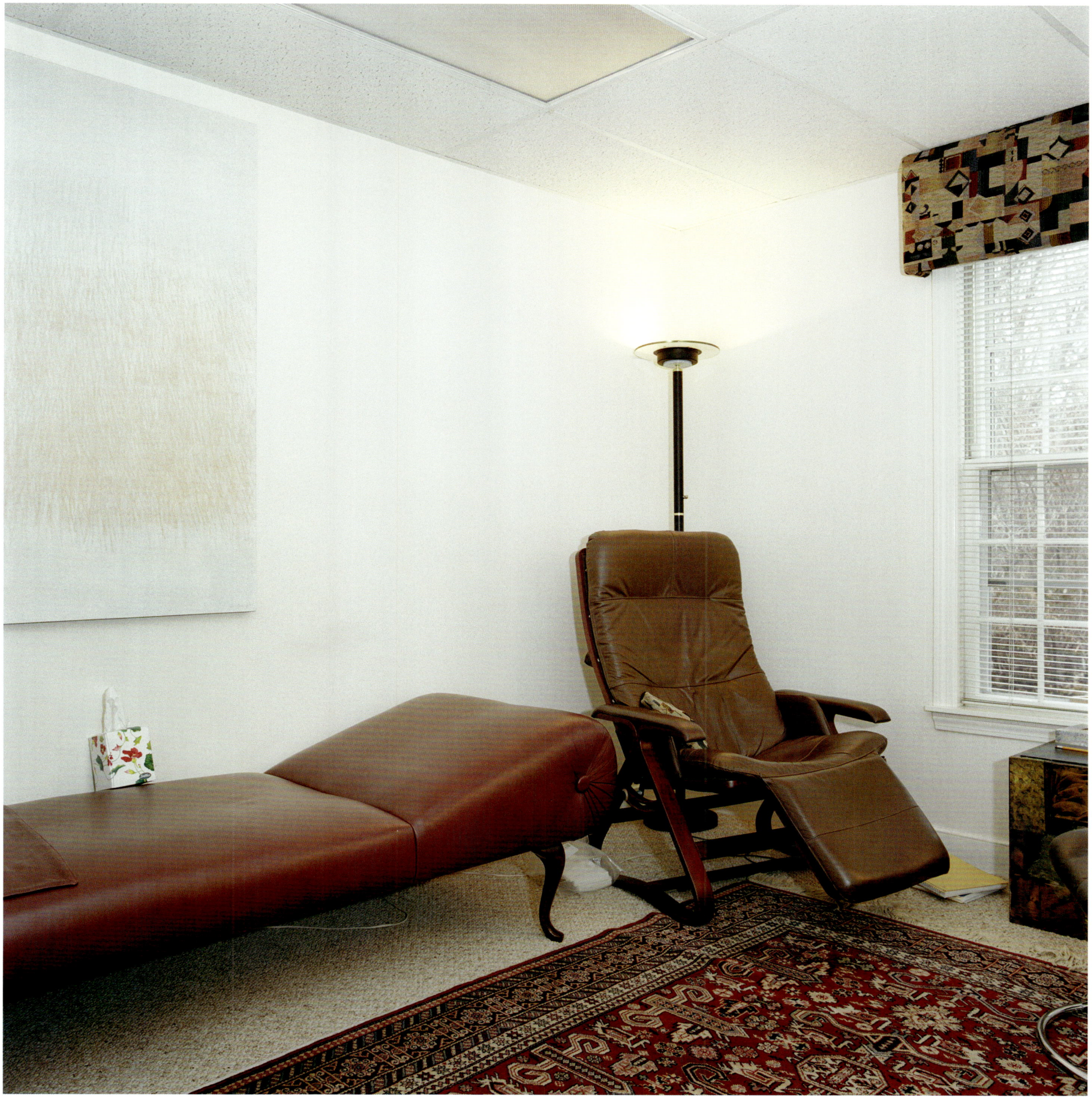

Brookline, MA

Office with Native American wall hanging, 2000

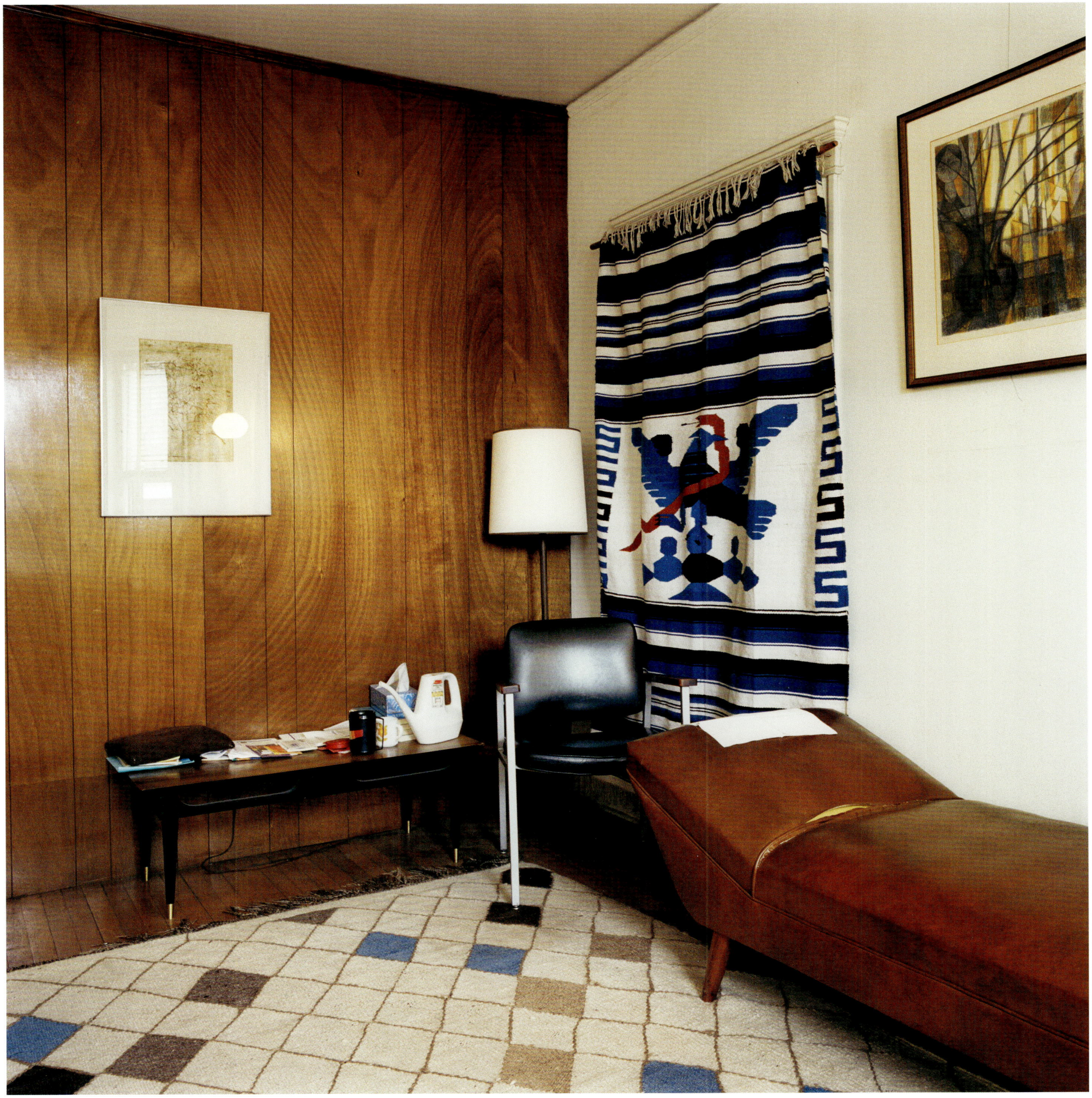

Brookline, MA
Hospital office with blue leather patient's chair and bookcase, 2000

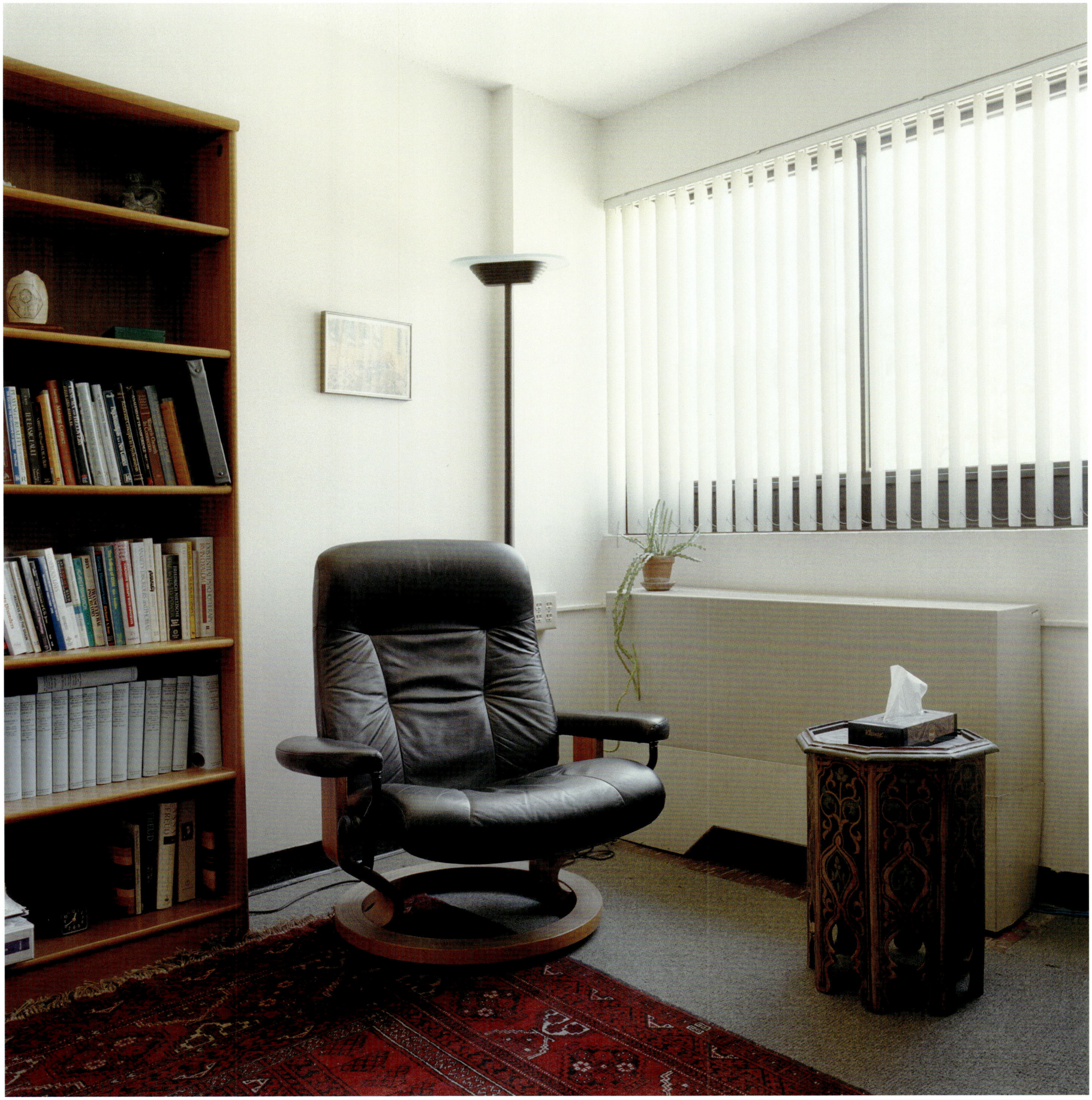

Buenos Aires
Office with glass door and red velvet analyst's chair, 1999

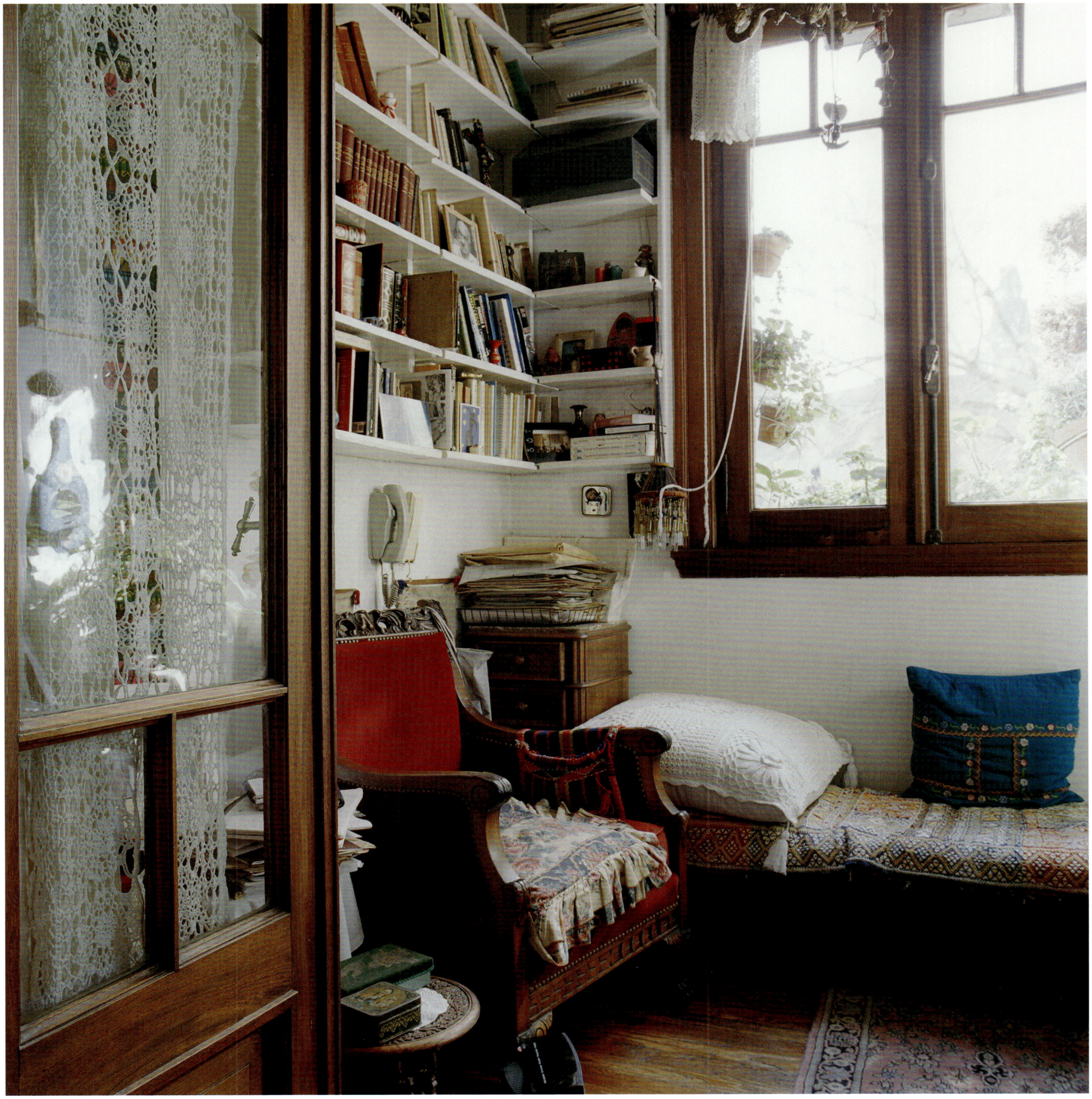

Brookline, MA

Office with red fabric couch and blue leather analyst's chair, 2000

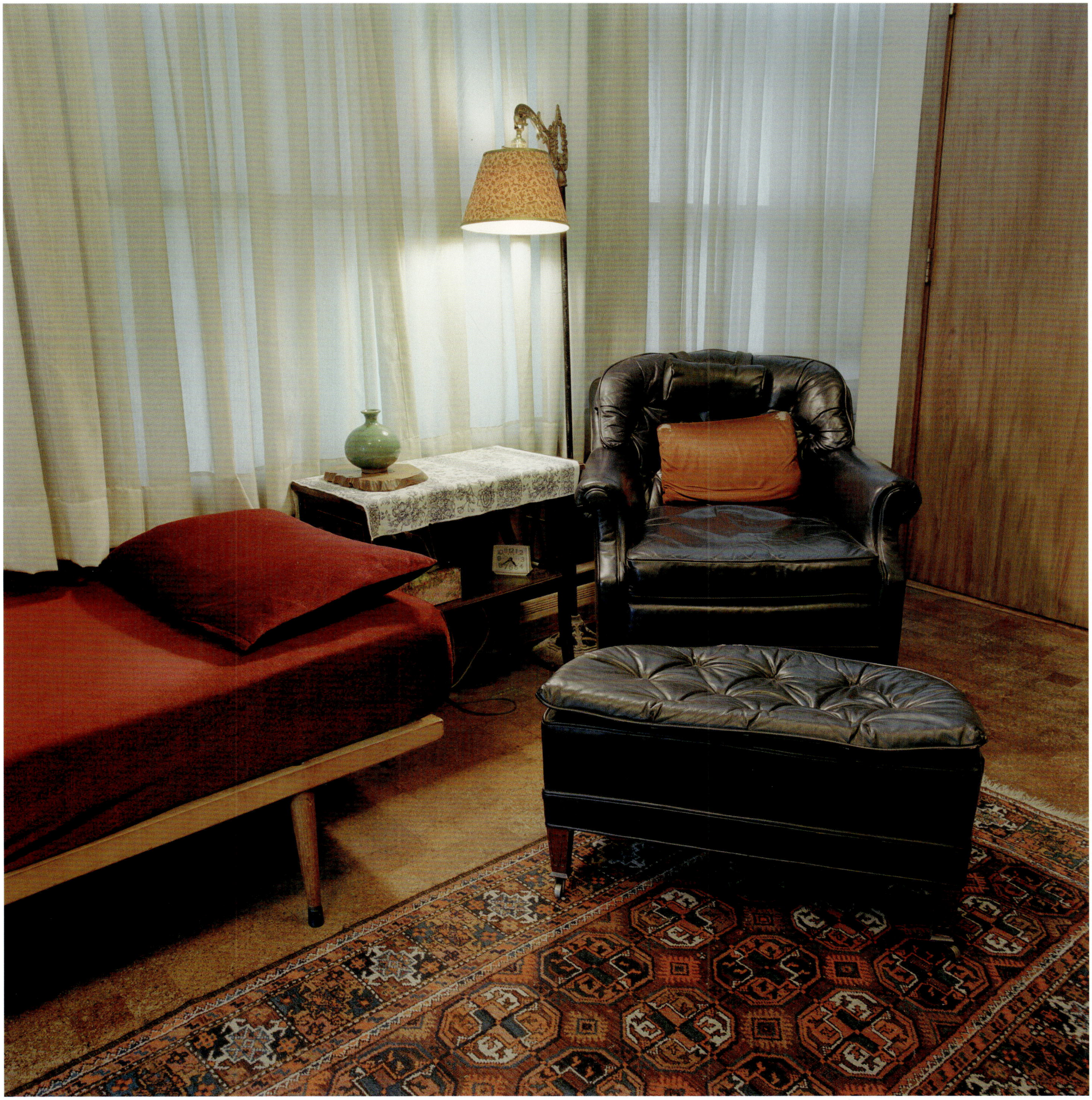

Newton, MA
Office with pink curtain and rattan screen, 2000

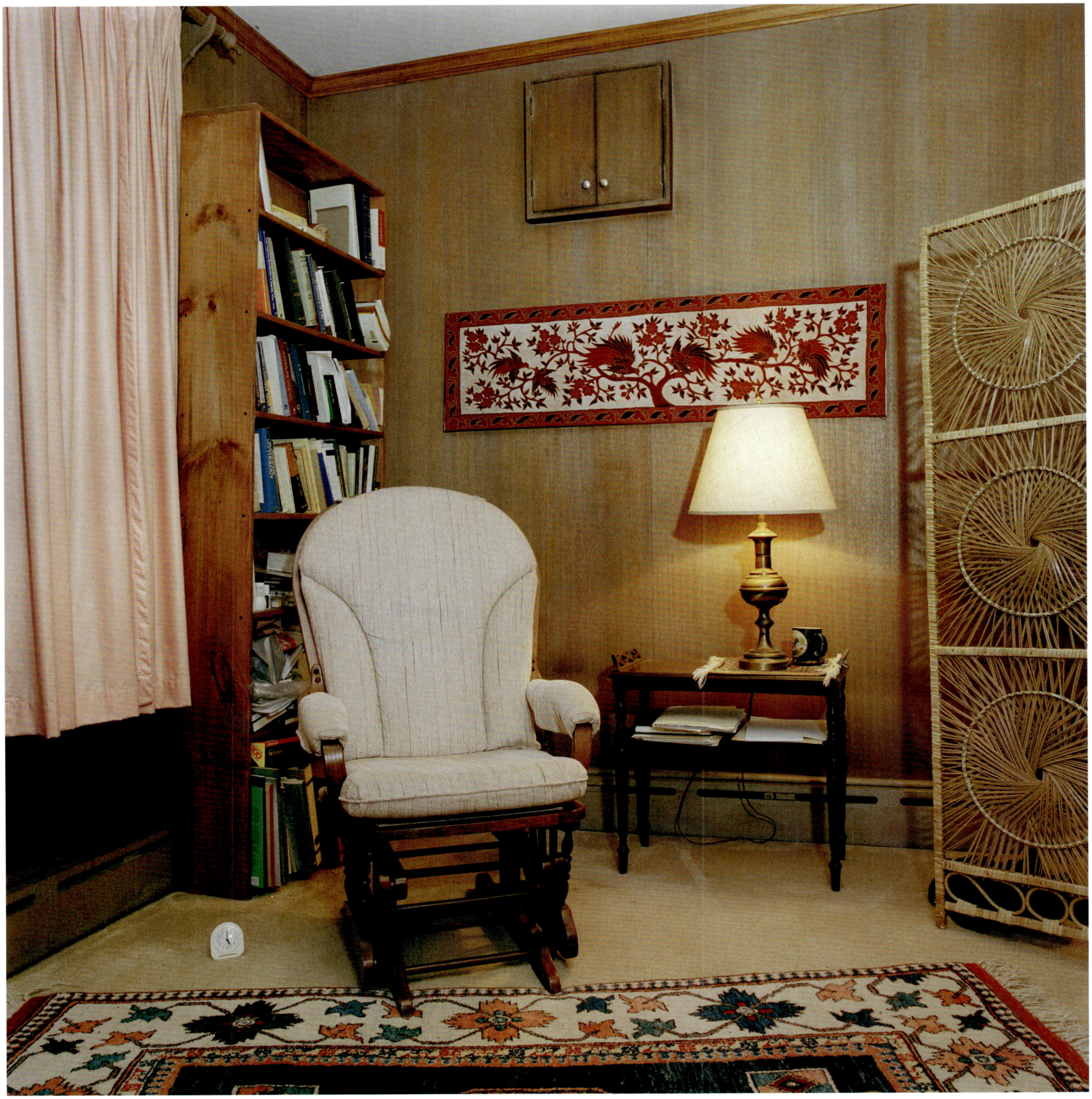

Newton, MA

Attic office with couch, chair and Palladian window, 2000

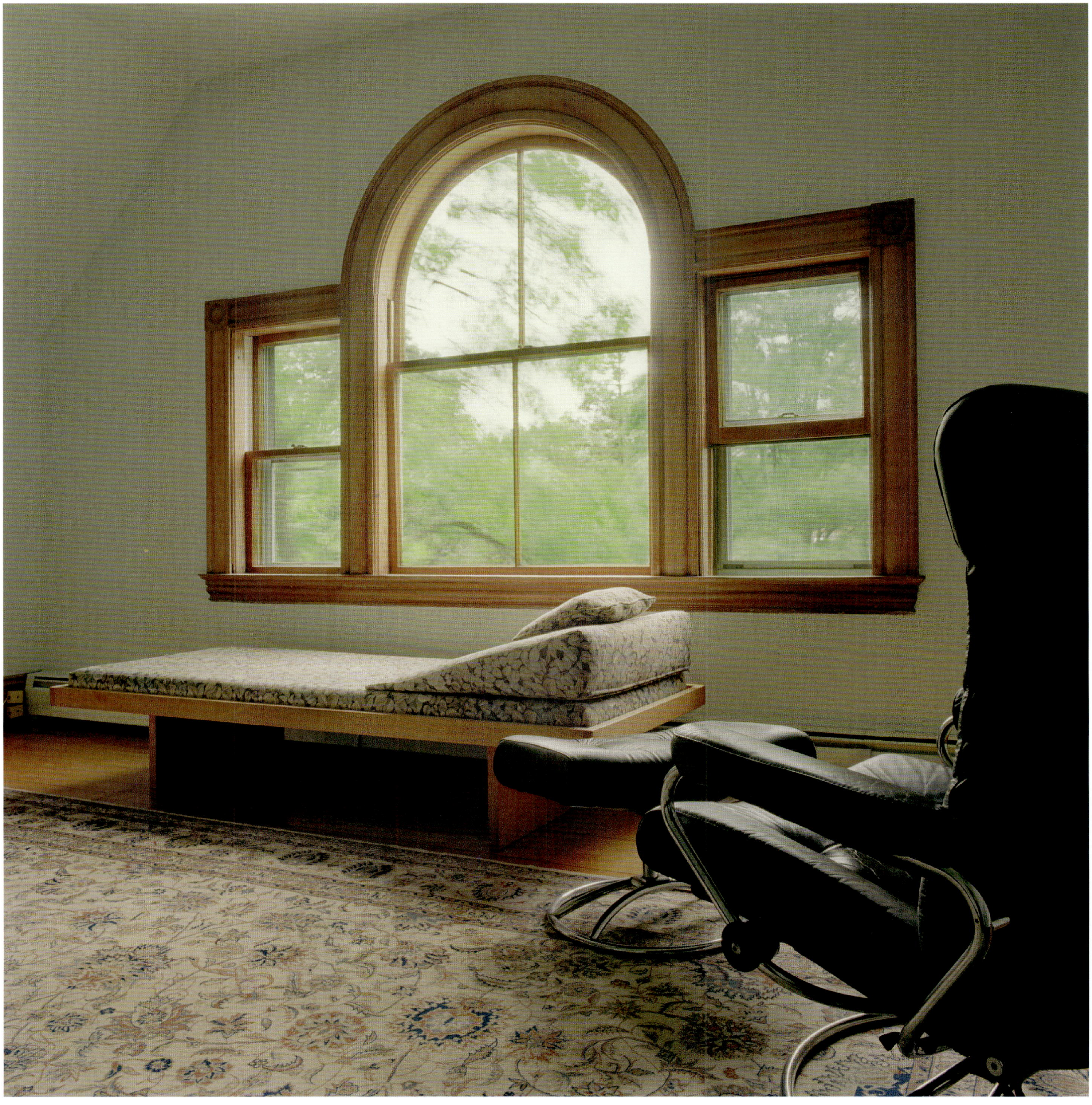

Arlington, MA
Office with red window curtain and small statuettes, 2000

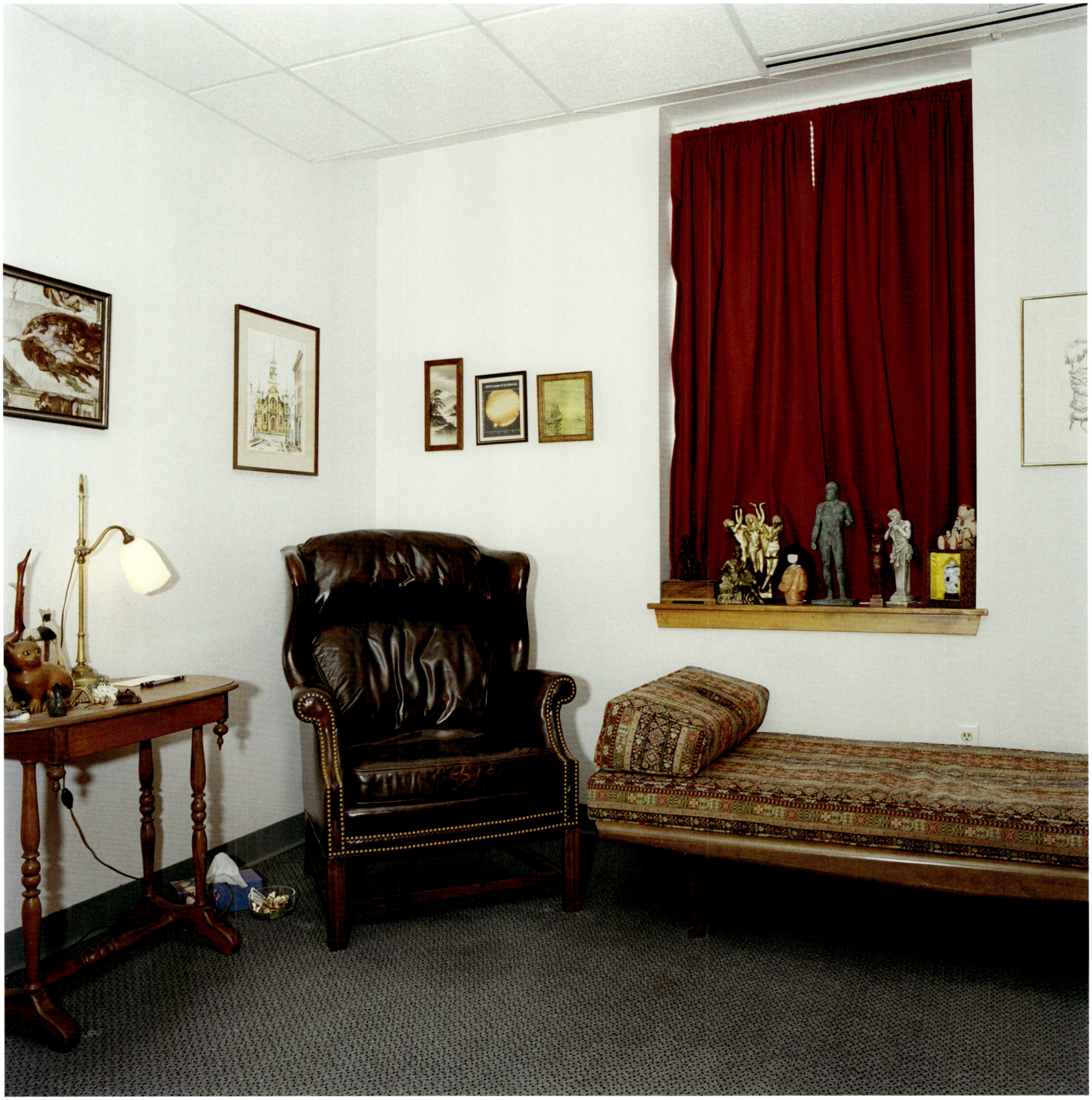

Cambridge, MA

Green overstuffed analyst's chair and leather footrest, 2000

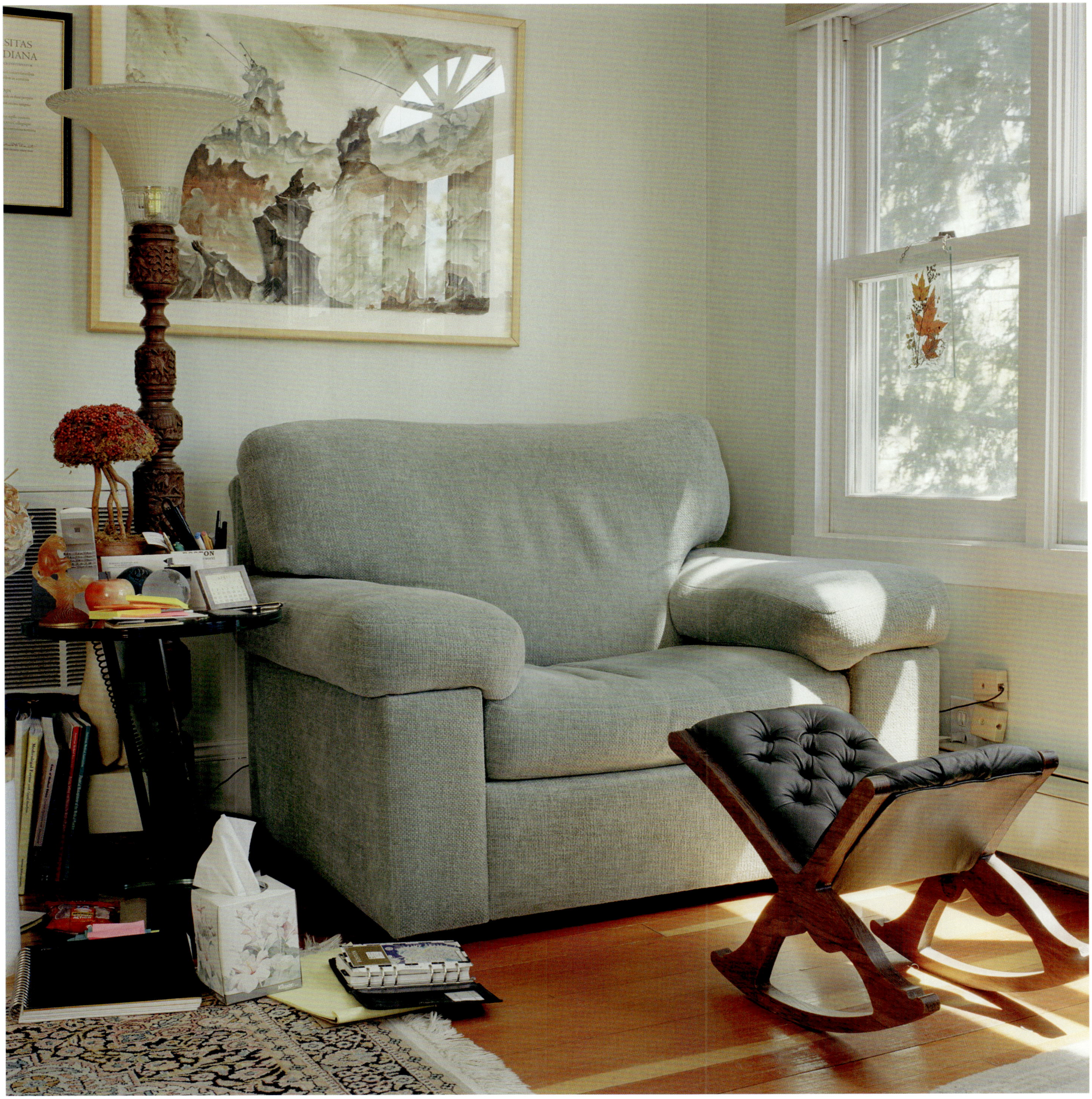

Newton, MA
Basement office with paisley fabric couch, 2000

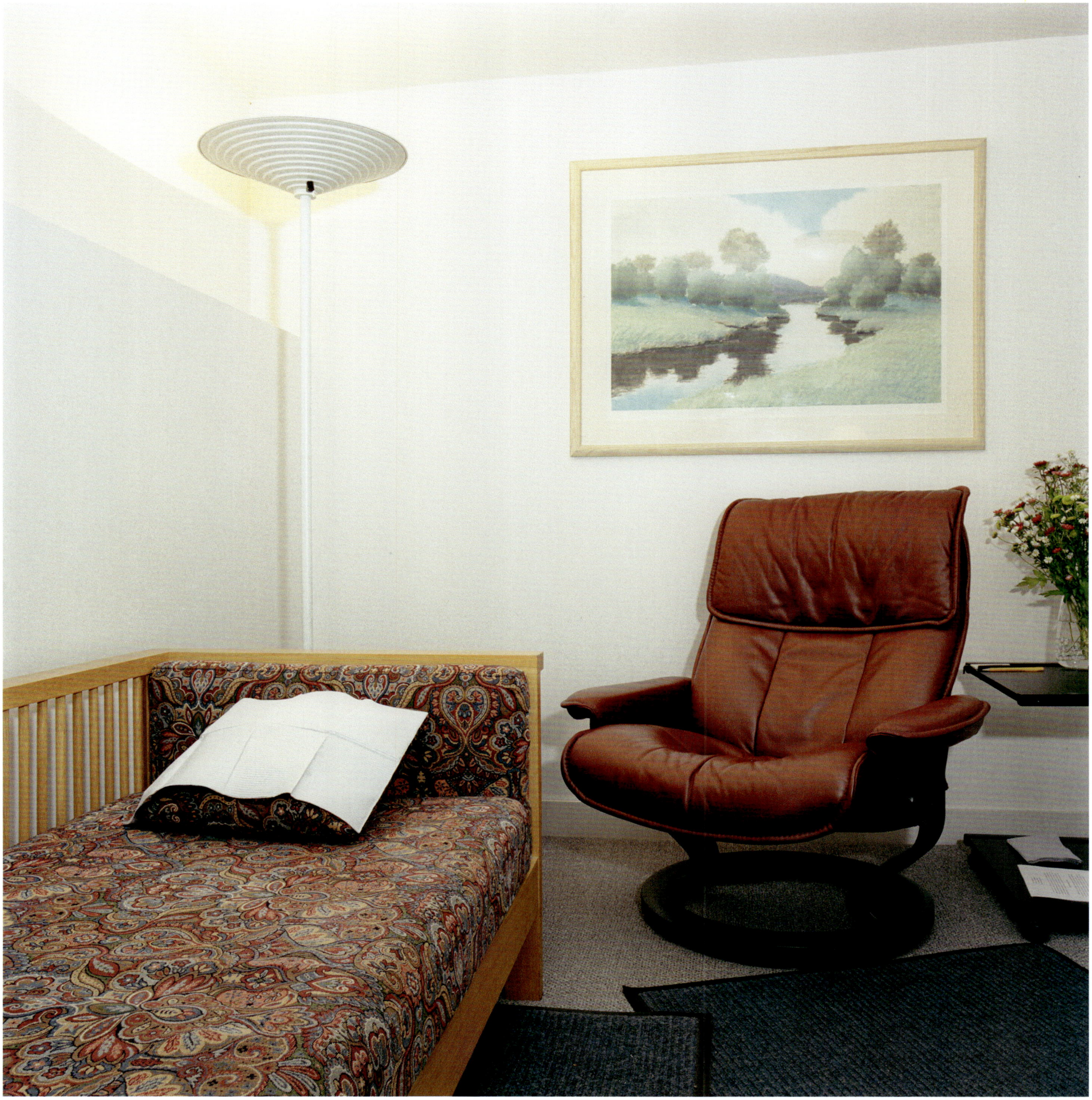

Boston, MA
Analyst's chair with painting of crooked house, 2000

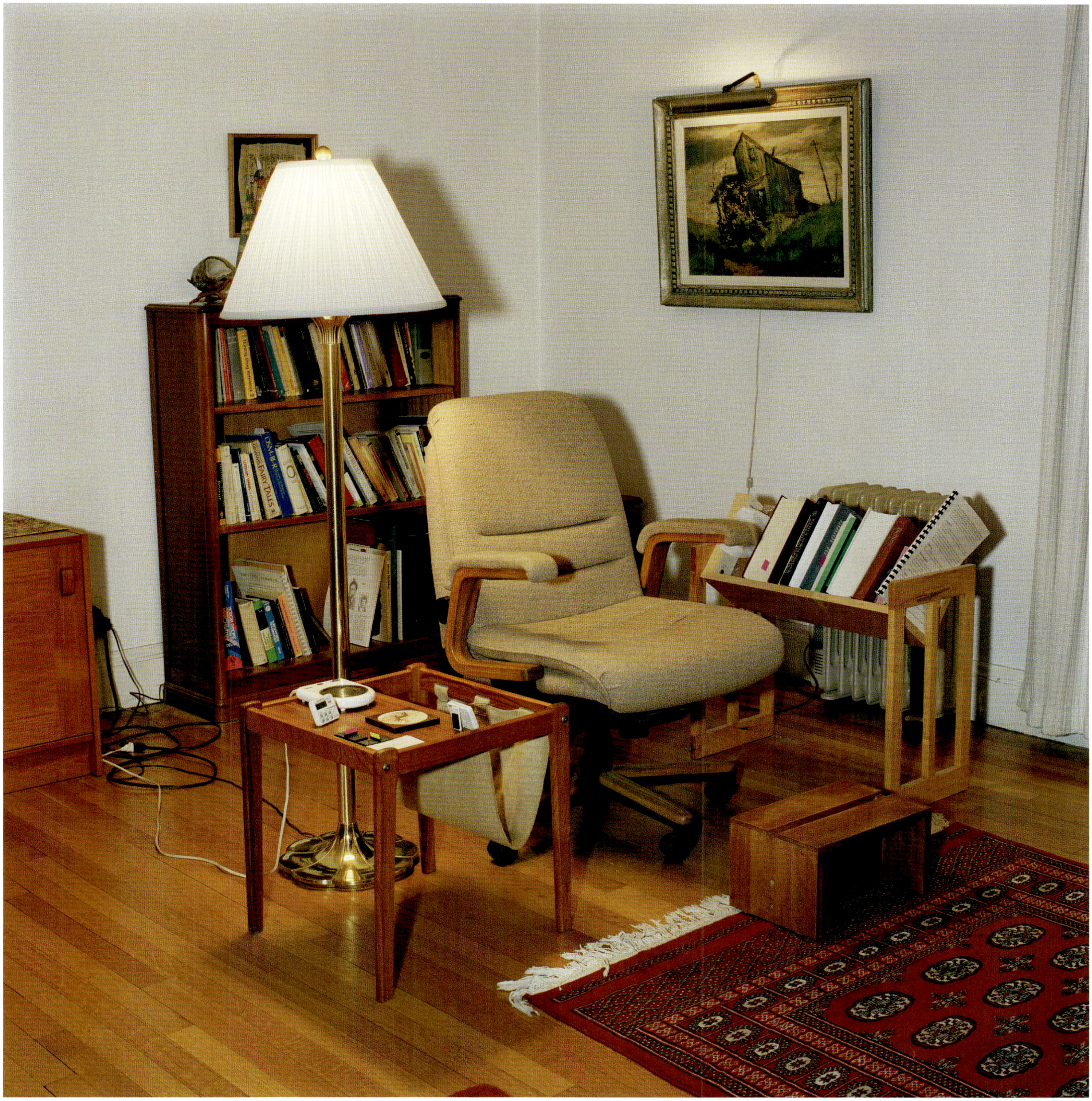
FAIRY TALES

Cambridge, MA

Office with Harvard chair and ochre-colored fabric couch, 2000

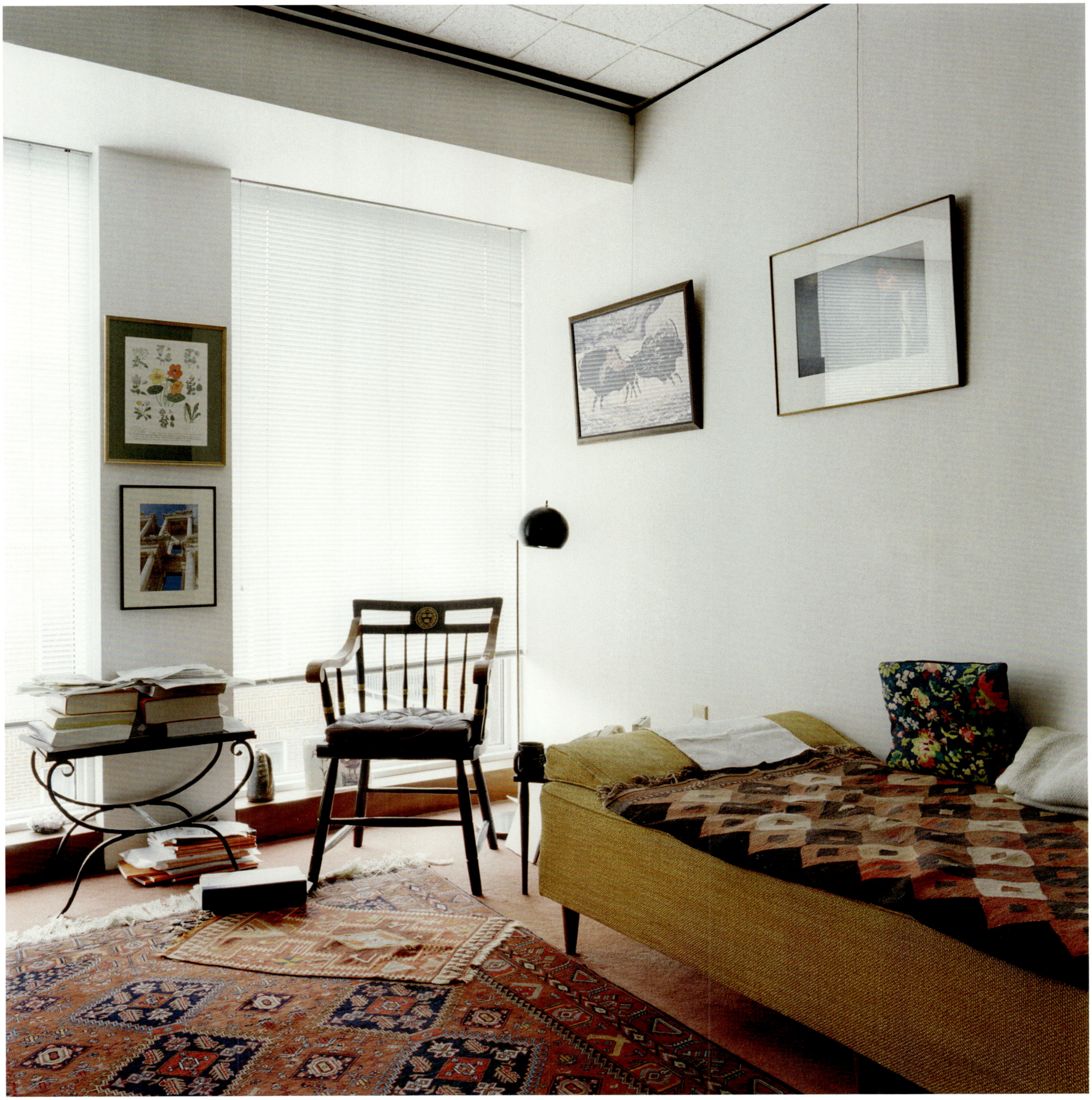

Jamaica Plain, MA

Office with tufted leather patient's chair and black wooden screen, 2000

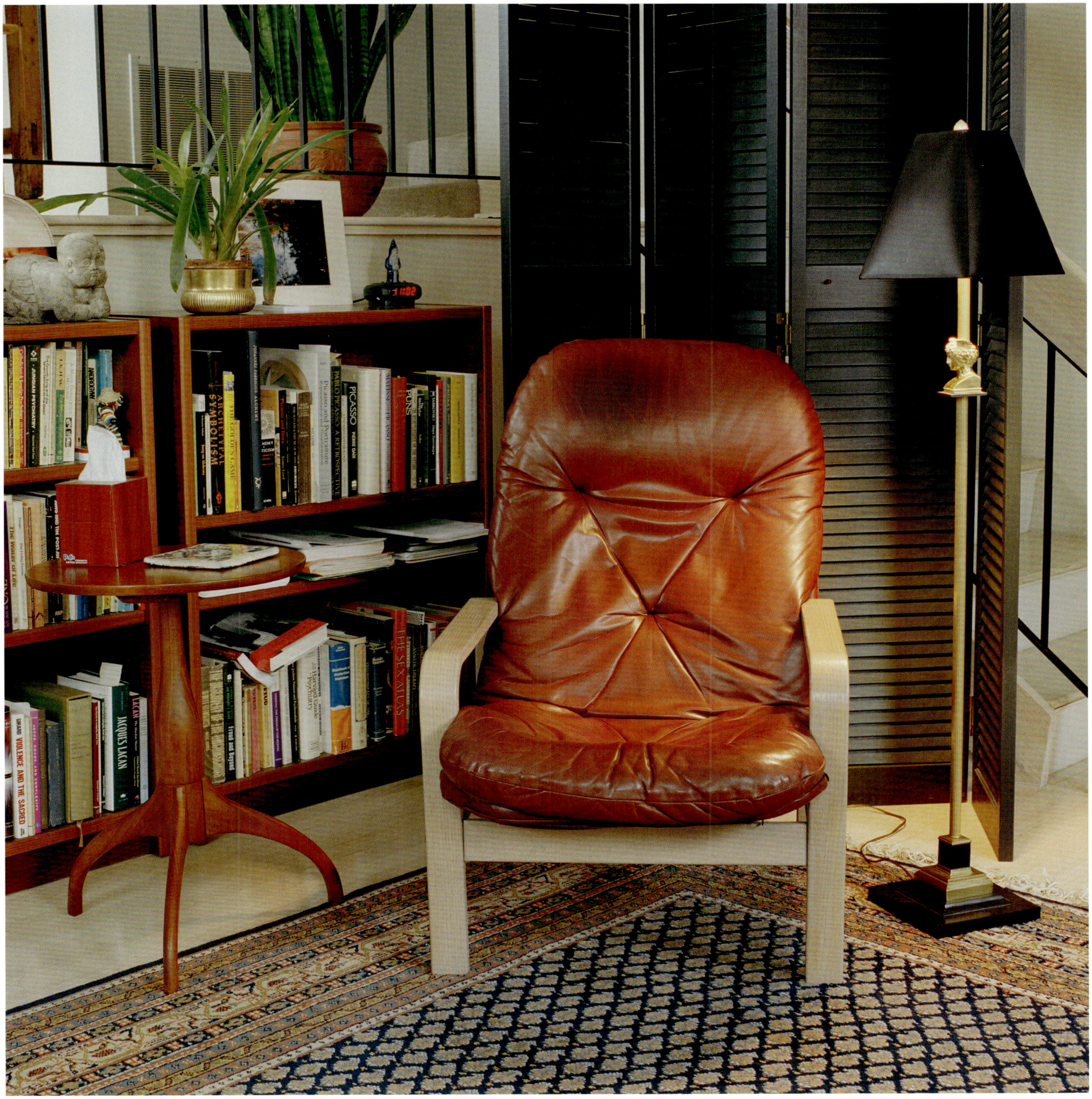
ARCHETYPAL SYMBOLISM
THE GOLDEN GAME
PICASSO
PABLO PICASSO A RETROSPECTIVE
JACQUES LACAN
VIOLENCE AND THE SACRED
THE SEX ATLAS
Freud and Beyond

Brookline, MA
Office with oriental rug on the wall, 2000

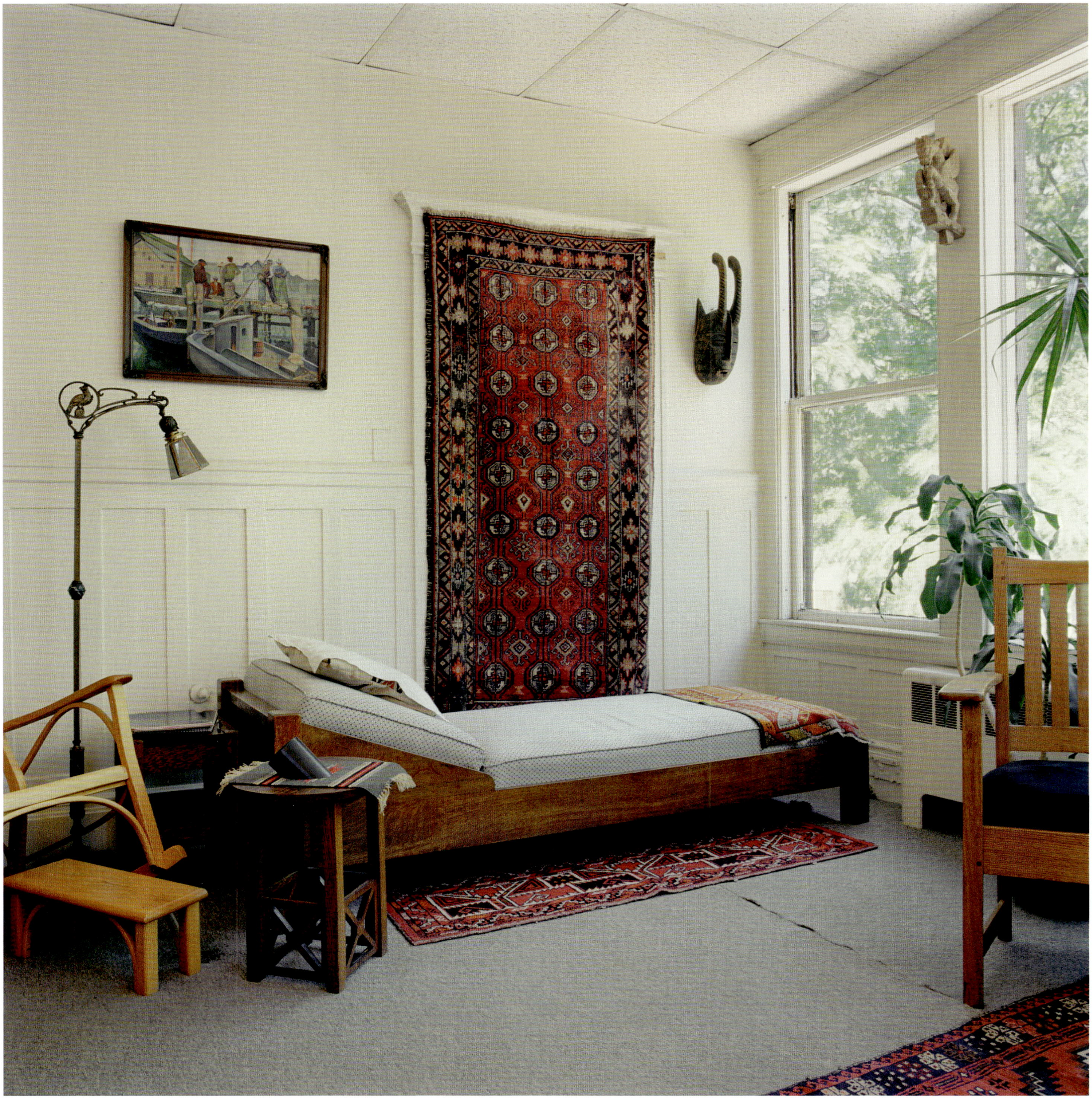

West Newton, MA
Office with overstuffed analyst’s chair and couch with red paper pillow protector, 2000

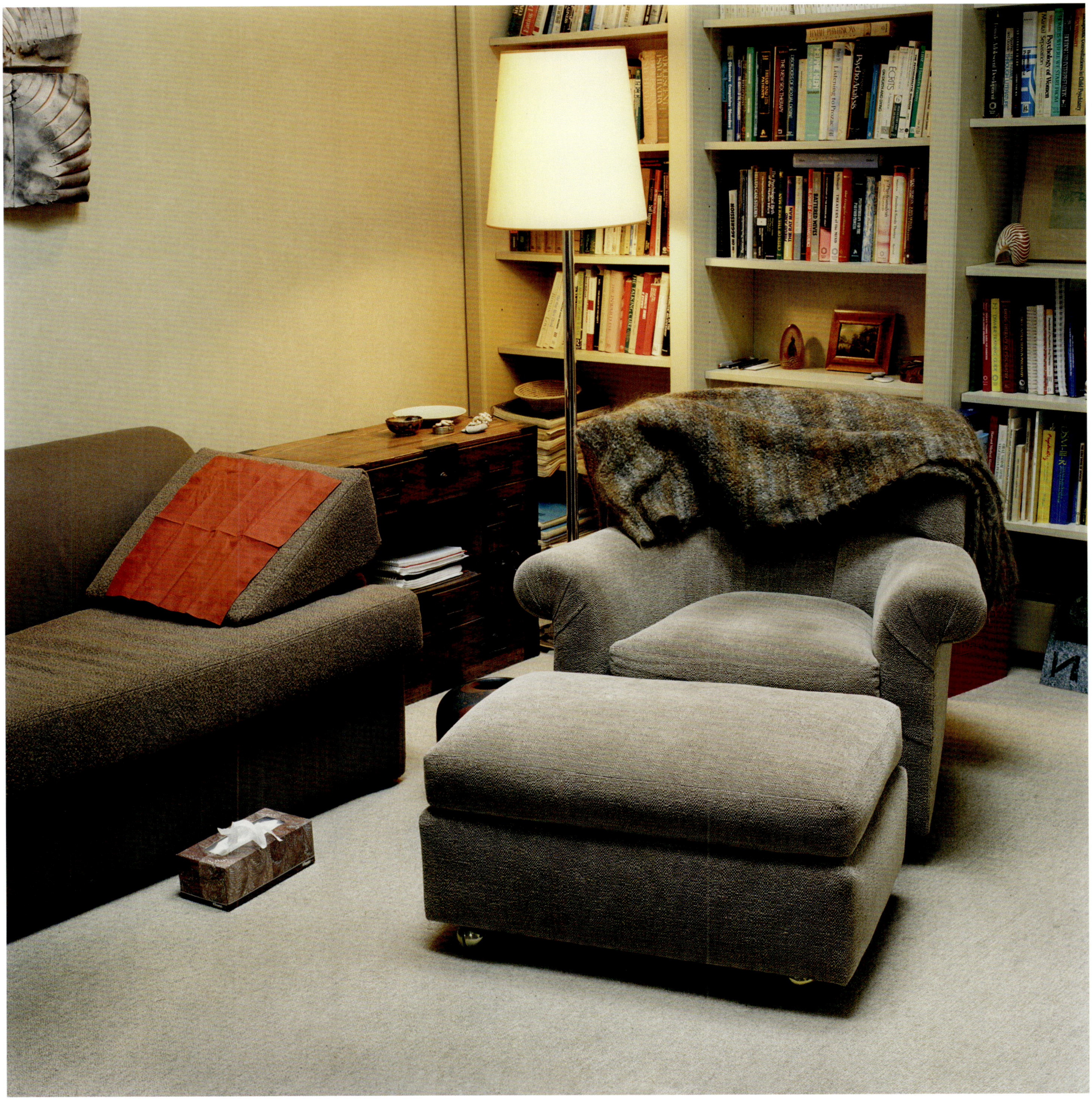
Obsessive Compulsive Disorders
FREUD AND HIS PATIENTS
THE NEW SEX THERAPY
DISORDERS OF SEXUAL DESIRE
Listening to Prozac
Psycho Analysis
ON DEATH AND DYING
ECRITS
THE PSYCHOANALYTIC DIALOGUE
Psychology of Women
Marital Separation
THROUGH LITERATURE
THEMES WHERE WE START FROM
Diagnostic Consultations in Child Psychiatry
ON AGGRESSION
FREUD'S CASE STUDIES
FREUD AND THE RAT MAN
BATTERED WIVES
TREATERS of the MIND

Jamaica Plain, MA
Analyst's desk with lamp and antique glass shade, 2000

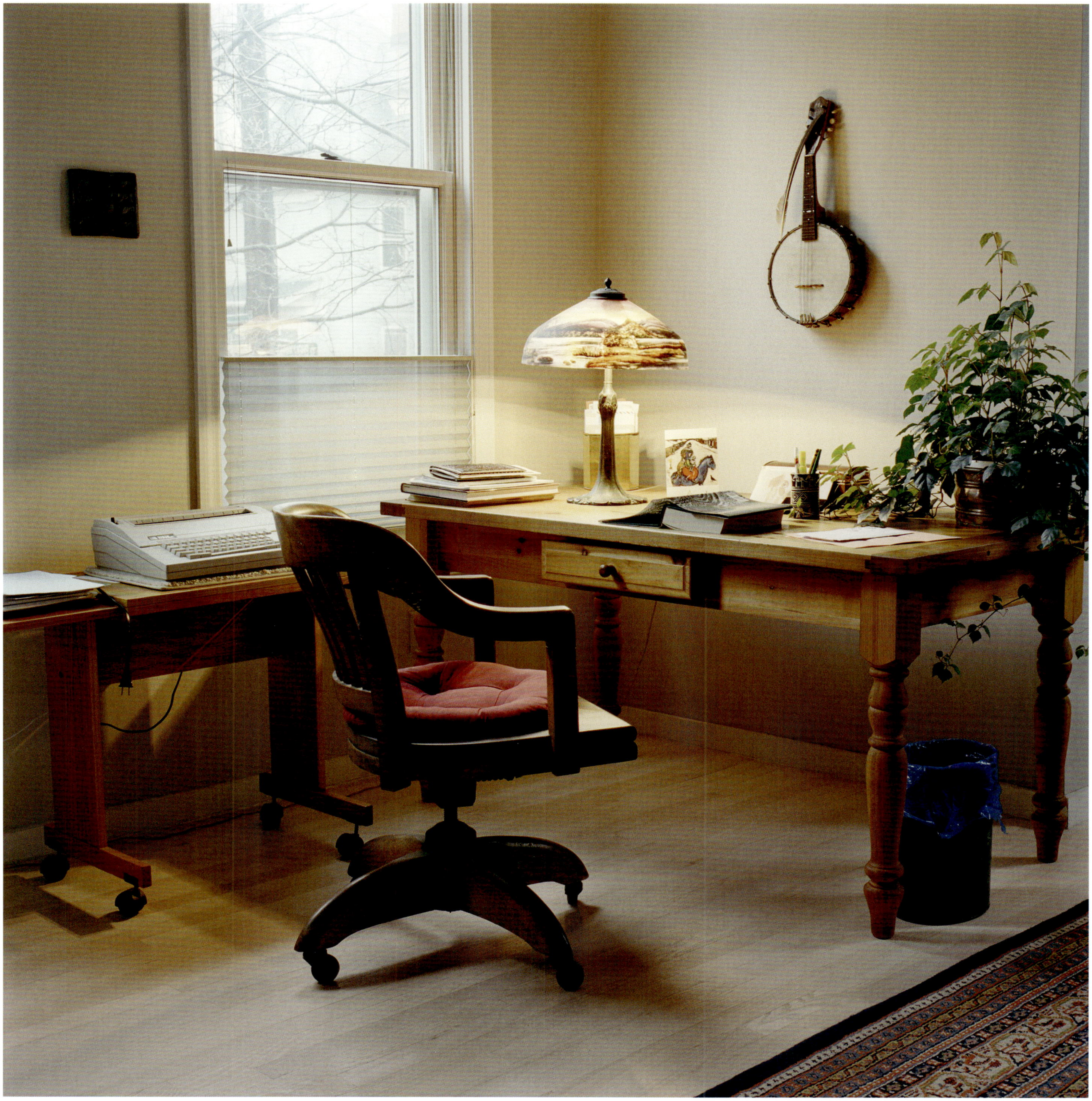

Boston, MA
Back Bay office with beige fabric couch, 2000

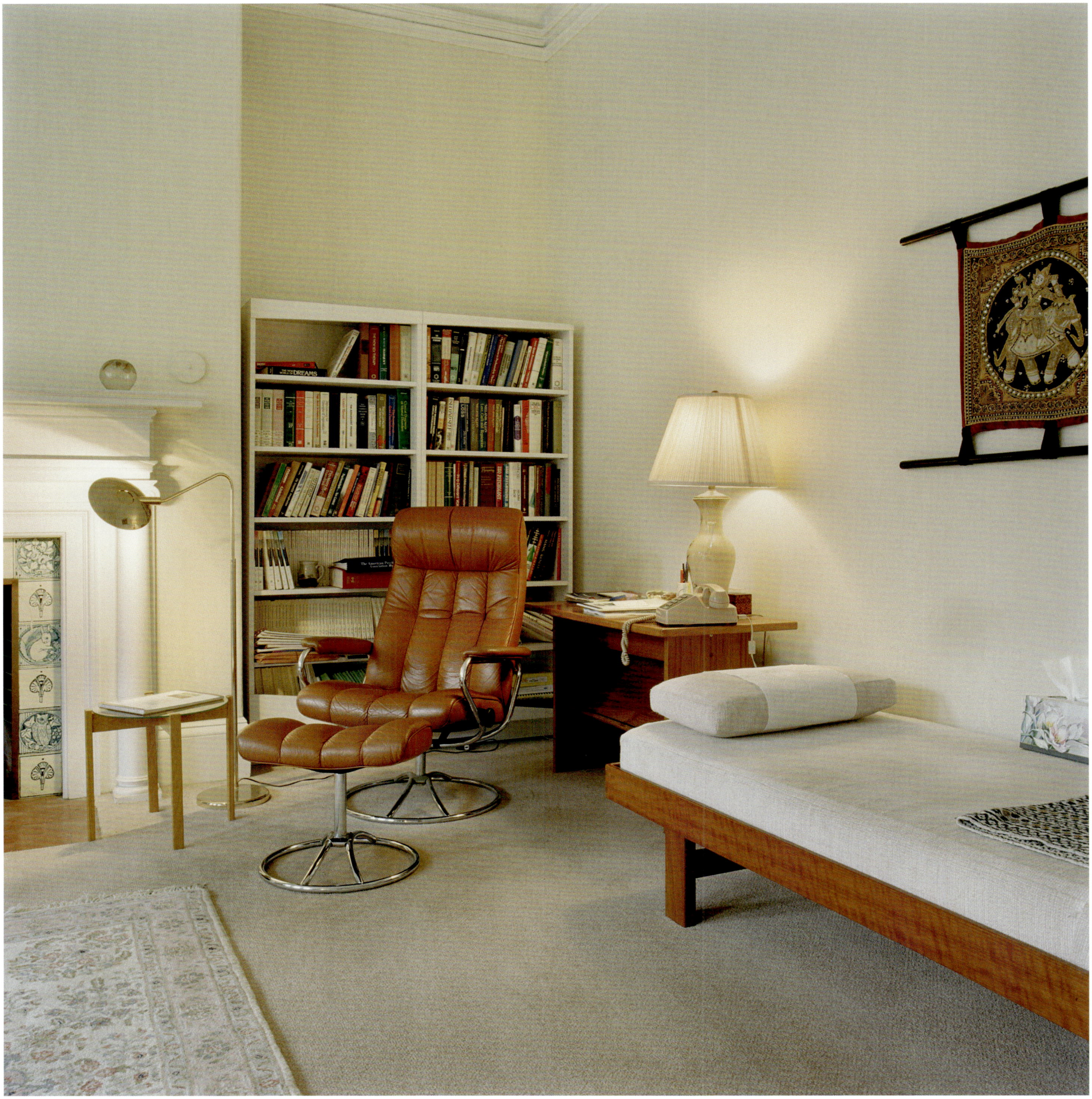

Brookline, MA
Office with blue leather chair and wooden Venetian blinds, 2000

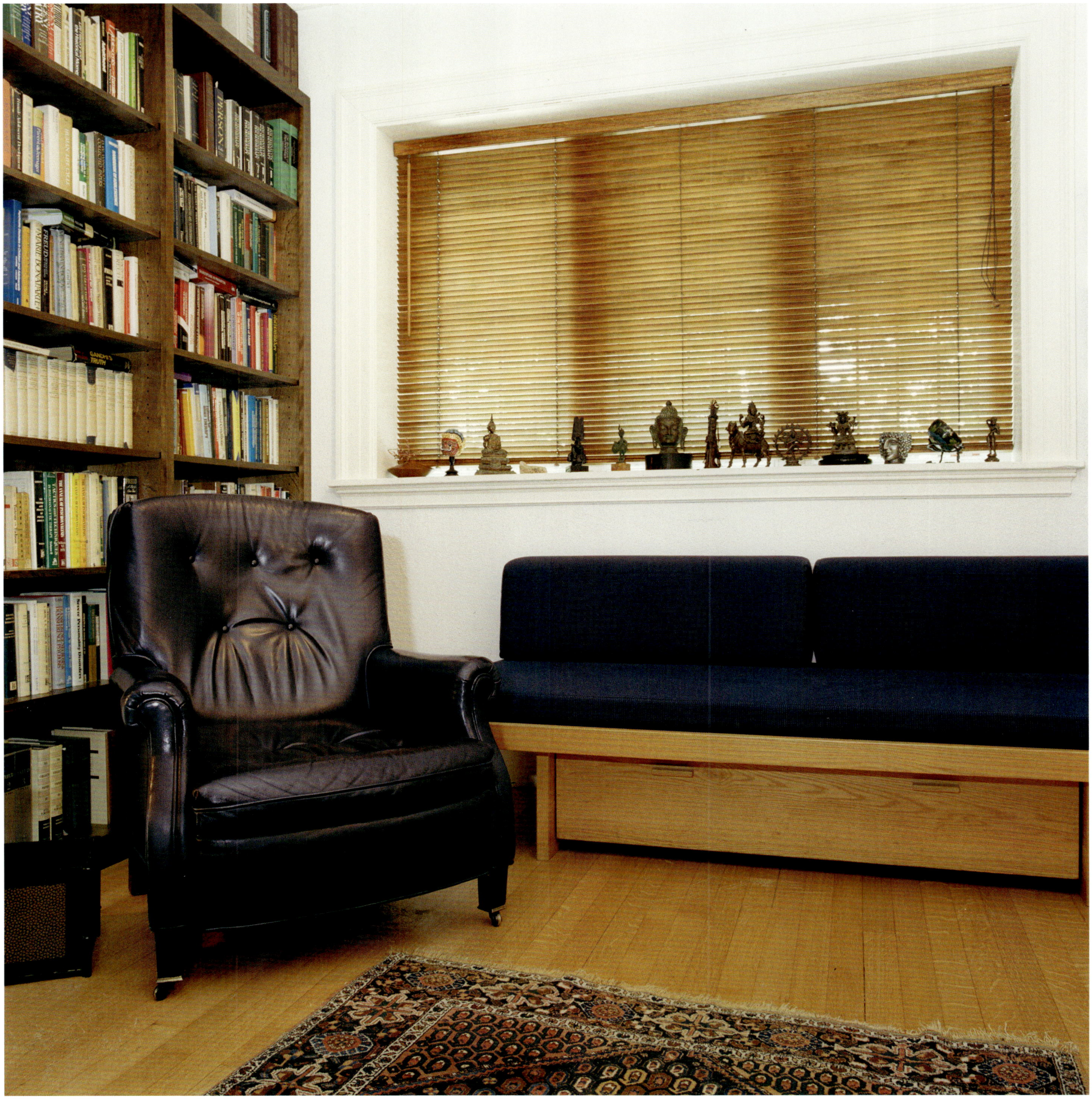

Brookline, MA
Office with soft fawn-colored fabric walls, 2000

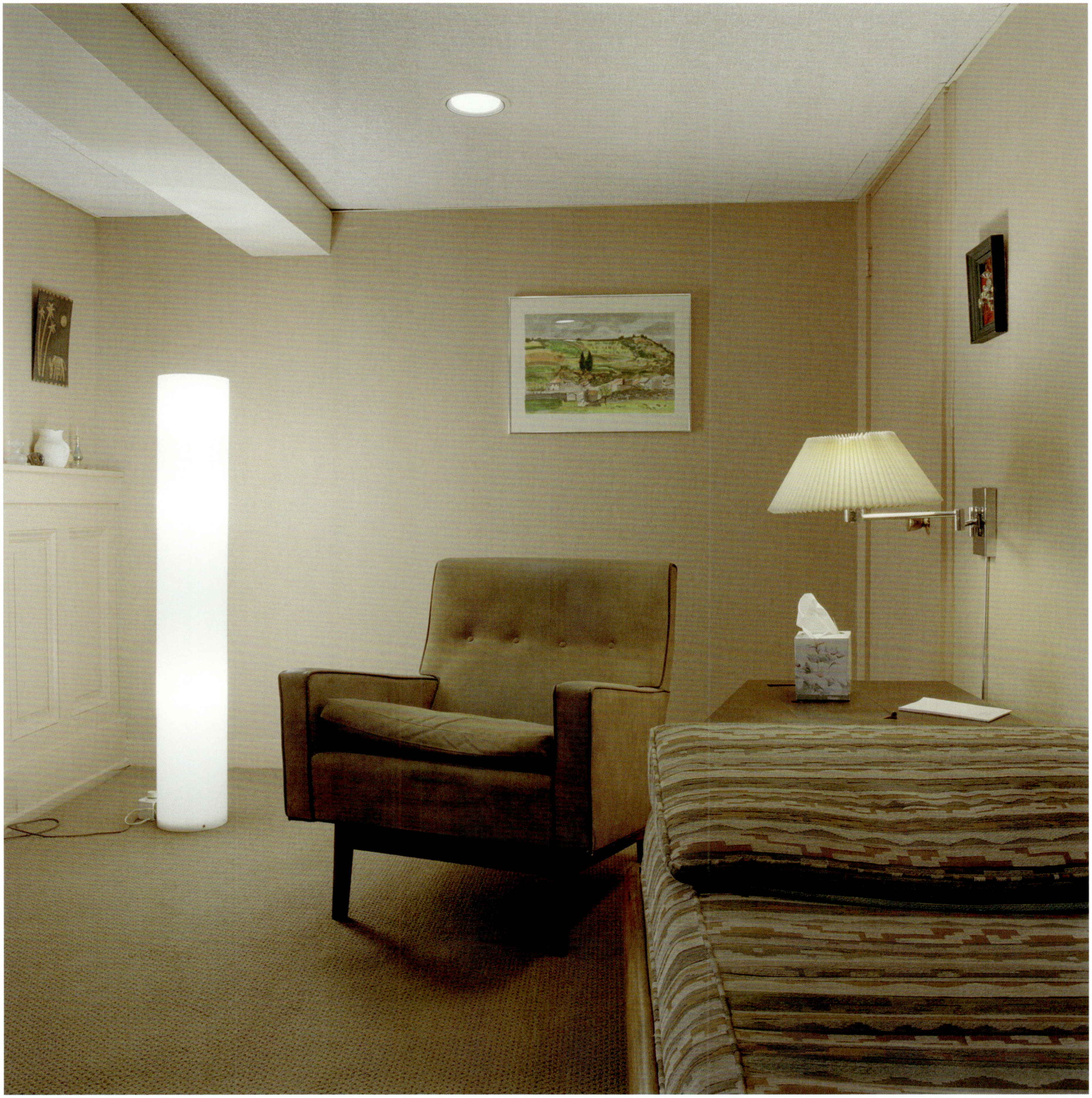

Buenos Aires
Analyst's desk with deep red velvet chair, 1999

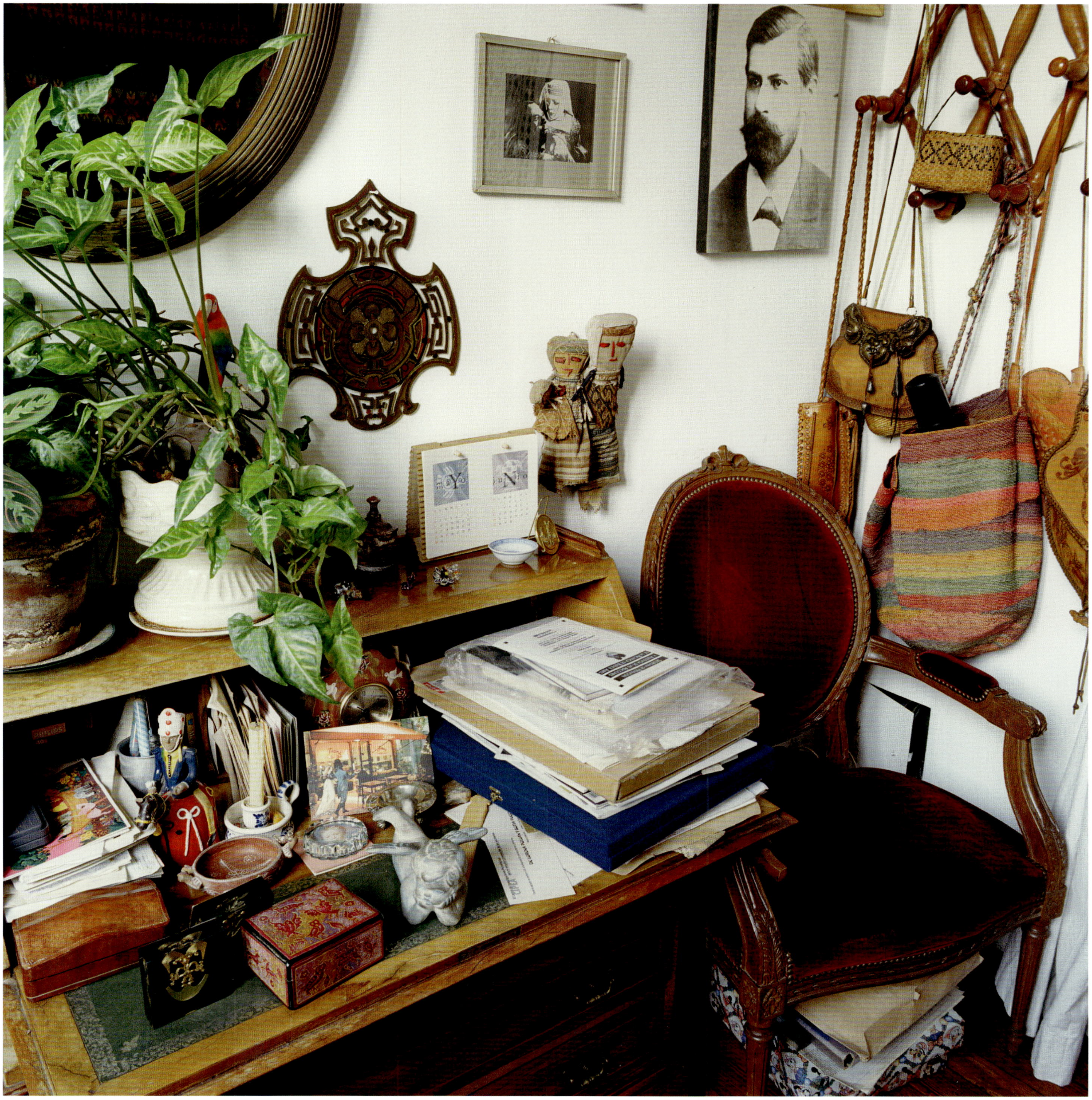

Buenos Aires
Analyst's desk with photographic portrait of Freud, 1999

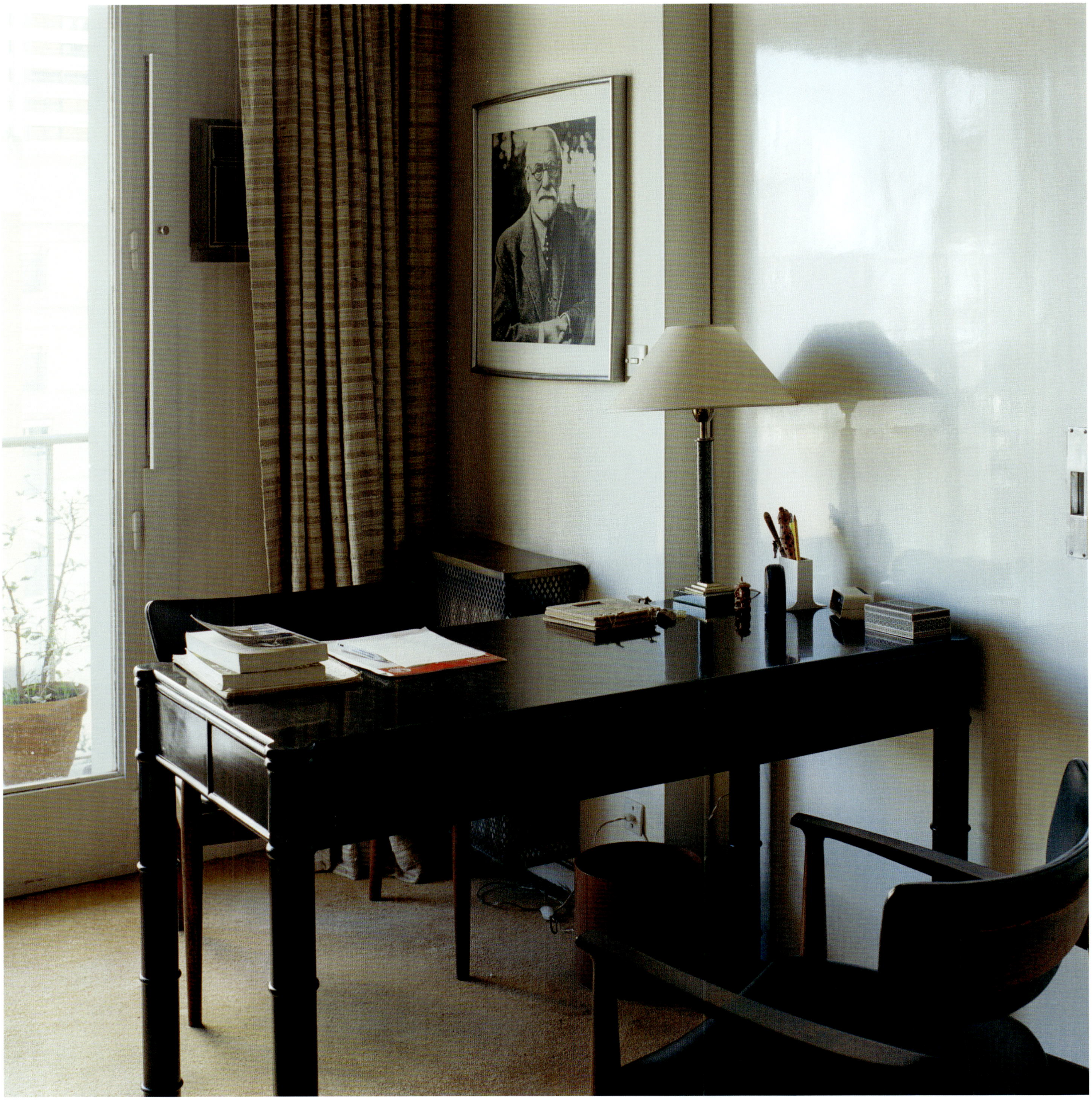

INTERVIEW WITH JESS T. DUGAN

Jess T. Dugan: You've had a long and varied career over the past fifty years, comprised of multiple projects and bodies of work. One could argue, of course, that they circle around a central set of questions and interests, which we'll get to shortly. Before we take a deeper dive into *Analysis*, I'd like to get a sense of context for your broader practice. So, briefly: what first led you to photography, and what was your path getting to where you are today?

Shellburne Thurber: It's hard to know exactly when and where I began. I started taking pictures in my late teens, and continued when I briefly attended Skidmore College. I entered the college with photos in hand that I had casually taken over the previous year or two. Soupy, overly sensitive self-portraits, close-ups of rocks and flowers, beach shots... that sort of thing. Awful stuff. But it was a start. Weirdly, the art department didn't have a photography class I could take, but the school did have a system with a fall and spring term, and then an interim winter term where you could fashion your own course. I decided to focus on photographing close-ups of distressed billboards... they kind of looked like Aaron Siskind photographs. I was interested in design at the time, and photographing abstractly appealed to me. In all honesty, it was also a way to get out of Dodge. I disingenuously argued at the time that the only way I could do this project was to move to Boston for the month and pursue the project there. A friend's father was a doctor in the Boston area and had a darkroom. I believe he was the one who taught me how to process film and make prints. My stint at Skidmore didn't last long and I ended up moving into Saratoga Springs, which was a great place to be living at the time (late sixties). I rented a room in a fabulous Stanford White-designed Victorian which had an unusual collection of residents. I was fairly lost due to the recent death my mother, who died very young of breast cancer. My fellow housemates became a kind of surrogate family. They also represented an alternative to the standard way of being in the world. In some ways, I felt like I had found my tribe: a motley crew who self-segregated in the house according to floor. Members of a New York state motorcycle club lived on the first floor, the jockeys who worked at the track lived on the second floor, the witches lived on the third, and a handful of artists lived on the top floor of the house. It was wild and lots of fun. At one point, I was giving drawing classes to the bikers who lived downstairs. I mention this time because I believe this is when I started to think about photography as something more than a hobby. The way it could record community and give evidence to my life felt important, considering how much my family lost when my mother died. This is also the point when I started photographing my family in a serious way, which I have continued to do to the present day.

JTD **I love hearing about your early days, and it's interesting to think about how your experience living in that house affected you. Much of your work focuses on the energy of space, whether it's a personal place, such as your family home, or an institutional space, such as the Boston Athenaeum. And, of course, this notion is deeply embedded within *Analysis*, which is all about the energy that exists in a particular space as the result of the people who have spent time there.**

Can you talk to me about this theme in your work? What originally led you to photograph spaces? How has your thinking about the energy of place shifted over time?

ST Shortly after my mother died, I began taking trips out to southern Indiana to see my grandmother. She lived in a Hopper-like house set on a hillock in the middle of vast cornfields. She was deeply depressed, having lost most of her family within a short span of time—her husband and two of her three children passed within a few years of each other. I was too mired in my own sadness around my mother's death and probably not mature enough to understand how devastating it must have been for her. She spent much of her time indoors with all the shades pulled. When she went to bed at night, I skulked around looking for something that would give me a clue into who my mother was—letters, school essays, well-loved dolls, that sort of thing—but as cluttered as the house was, it was weirdly devoid of anything personal. And then it hit me that the house itself was the clue. In some ways, it said more about my mother and the way she grew up than any childhood trinket or other type of memento could. I shot a few rolls and when I got back to Boston and looked at them, I knew I had stumbled onto something interesting. Certainly, I never intended to pursue this line of inquiry, but I always had my camera with me and it just kind of happened. I had mostly been taking pictures of people up to that point, and continued to do so, but looking at the pictures of the house my mother grew up in, I realized space could speak to character in a way that straight up portraiture couldn't. I've always felt that portraiture is more about the photographer anyway. Not that it doesn't capture something true about the sitter, but it's always mediated through the eye of the person behind the camera. This fascination with space continued when I took pictures of my Aunt Anna's house shortly after she died. We were very close and I wanted to photograph the house in an effort to preserve my memory of her. I took a set in black and white of the house furnished, and then another set after it was emptied out. Interestingly, the color shots of the empty house were so much more evocative and truer to my aunt's nature. The light streaming in through the windows became her, in some sense. And as I looked at them, I felt that I had captured her energy in a way that I couldn't with the furnished ones, which struck me as looking slightly funereal. It was almost as if her belongings were weighing her down, and without them she was free to be purely herself. From that point on, I was on a roll. I photographed abandoned homes in North Carolina, sacred spaces in the Adirondack State Park, and the Boston Athenaeum (as you mentioned), to name a few. Over time, what became clear to me was that except for private domiciles, most space is an interesting mix of public and private, and it's this intersection of the two that really intrigues me.

JTD **Let's talk specifically about *Analysis*. How did this project begin? What drew you to photograph the offices of psychoanalysts?**

ST I began this project in Buenos Aires when I visited with my friend Jim Dow for a few weeks. He'd been photographing in Argentina for a number of years. We stayed with Gela Rosenthal, a friend of his who was an analyst. When I asked her if I could photograph her office, she immediately agreed and offered to set me up with several of her friends who were amenable to letting me record their consulting rooms. Once I got home, I continued the project here in the Boston area, where there is a strong and thriving analytic community. I had received a fellowship from the Radcliffe Institute for Advanced Study, which gave me financial support and a free year to pursue this project. It also gave me the credentials I needed to approach these people in the first place. Interestingly, I had been working with an analytically-inclined therapist for years, so I had been primed for this project by the work we had been doing. I've been fascinated by psychoanalysis for a long time, both in terms of how it has shaped the way we view ourselves, and the way that it has influenced many artists over the last several decades.

As I've mentioned, I'm also really interested in spaces that are both public and private, and analytic spaces are a perfect example of this. These offices are often located in the analyst's home and contain all sorts of objects that are weighted in meaning for the practitioner. As the patient, you quickly come to see the space as yours for the fifty minutes you are in it, forgetting that most likely, many other people think of it the same way you do. The space becomes part of the analysis, in a way: a site of projection. These offices are, from an energetic standpoint, complicated for exactly this reason—you have so many people and histories colliding in one spot. And as a clue into the nature of the analyst, these spaces are intriguing. Some are cluttered and look like they've been lived in for decades. Others are very spare and give little insight into the personality of the person they belong to. I'm reminded of a story an analyst in New Haven told me. A prospective patient had made an appointment to meet her to determine if she was someone the patient could work with. Apparently the two of them got along well, but the patient had a difficult time with the couch, finding it too soft. She eventually chose an analyst down the hall with a couch that was firm and sturdy. The patient told the first analyst that her couch felt too much like sinking into the lap of her suffocating mother.

JTD **Tell me more about your own experiences with psychoanalysis. I'm interested in the idea that psychoanalysis has affected the way we view ourselves, both individually and collectively, as well as the direct influence psychoanalysis has had on the work of artists. How have your experiences with analysis affected how you view yourself?**

ST I am not a student or expert on psychoanalysis by any means, but I feel I can speak to this topic in a general sort of way. Before Freud and all the analysts who came up with him, our notion of the mind was, if not non-existent, certainly very different. The way I see it, the advent of psychoanalysis brought with it a sense of interiority and self-consciousness, along with the idea that mind and body were interconnected. It was a way to lend some structure to inchoate thoughts and symptoms. In most cultures, wherever talk therapy is practiced, there is a good chance that the practitioners have been trained in analytic theory to some extent. Certainly there are many therapists who apply other modalities to their practices, but it would be hard to get through any kind of therapeutic training without a cursory introduction to psychoanalysis. Of course, many psychiatric disorders are treated with drugs now. The talking cure is expensive and doesn't fit in well with people's busy schedules and pocketbooks. I also think that in this era of quick fixes, the process can be slow, and most people want their problems to disappear quickly. The thing is, from my viewpoint, there's never been a time when good, in-depth therapy is needed more than in this moment, as evidenced by the fact that therapists are hard to find right now. But this is getting a little off topic.

Two of my favorite artists, Louise Bourgeois and Leonora Carrington, address psychoanalysis directly in their work and their writings. Jackson Pollock and Joan Miró come to mind as well. The Surrealism movement was heavily influenced by Freud. Much of their approach was predicated on freeing the subconscious from the normal filters and constraints of the rational mind, automatic drawing and the exquisite corpse technique being two well-known methods used for this purpose.

Personally, I never had any intention of going into analysis. It just so happened that the therapist I ended up with was a psychoanalyst, and the work we did was clearly shaped by this approach.

When I first started working with him, I wasn't quite sure what was going on. I had been in therapy before and was used to a problem-solving approach to whatever it was I brought to the table. Instead, after a brief intake interview, he sat back and waited for me to begin. It was uncomfortable. I had been anticipating a barrage of questions, some interest in why I had sought him out for help. Instead, he calmly sat back and waited for me to talk. It went on like this for several meetings. He wasn't completely silent, but the aural space was unnerving to say the least. It wasn't until long after we began that I realized that there was a method to his madness. Every session was carefully calibrated. Much like a good jazz musician, he would deftly take the temperature of the session and, if necessary, shift gears. We would then talk about another subject, mostly photography. He was a photographer himself, and it was a relief to be able to navigate terrain I was familiar with. He was smart and had a great eye. He often looked at my work, or helped me with grant proposals or exhibition questions. He was also my biggest cheerleader. He struck just the right balance. At one point I asked him why he felt it was helpful to just sit there and stare. He replied that he didn't experience it that way. Instead, he felt that he was giving me the gift of space to explore my thoughts. I didn't buy it at first, but I now realize that it was indeed an amazing gift. The problem was that I wasn't used to being listened to so intensely and I didn't know how to deal with it. Of course, he would weigh in when needed, but for the most part, he was there to witness, and by witnessing my life as it unfolded over all those years, both before and during our time together, he helped me form a different and more positive relationship to myself and my work. He was also like my external hard drive: his memory was unbelievable. Sometimes we would have minor squabbles about this. I would remember something one way and he would insist that it was another. I think I always eventually gave in to his view because he would almost always turn out to be right.

The analytic project might not have happened if it hadn't been for my work with him. It was a little like treading on his turf. I think my attraction to it was, in part, driven by a deep curiosity about this strange process I had embarked on, and the person I was working with.

It's funny though... I went to dinner one night with a few analysts when I was in the midst of this project and one of them turned to me and said, "You'd better watch out, if you take on too much therapy, you'll lose the impetus to do your work." I thought at the time that it was a strange and somewhat troublesome thing to say, but some deep part of me realized that I had worried about that very thing. It was clear to me that my work, especially the interior work, was driven by a need to figure something out, to express something that needed a voice. His remark hit a raw nerve because I had also wondered whether I might lose the drive to make my work if I became too self-aware. In actuality, I don't think there is such a thing as being "cured," so there is always going to be a need to search. I think that's what we human beings do. We are psychically, intellectually and emotionally driven to make sense of our time here, and I think that's where some of the impetus to make art comes from. It comes from a place that needs to make order.

Interestingly, I think I landed in my therapist's office in part because of the space itself. Initially, I had no intention of working with him. I had originally gone in for a consult, but between his sense of humor and the office, I ended up committing... signing on the dotted line. I was also struck by the fact that he had a framed poster of a painting done by one of my closest friends. I took that as a sign. The space was lovely. It sat on the corner of a busy street in a brownstone with two large cherry trees that sat just beyond the windows. I had a view of them as well as the street from where I sat. When things would get a little intense, I had something I could look at, a view I could get lost in, especially in the spring when the trees would break out in a cloud of white blossoms. I also liked being up high; I felt like I was sitting in a treehouse. The height felt safe—It made me think of the turkeys in my neighborhood that would lift themselves into the trees at night to sleep protected from possible predators.

At some point, he moved to another town and having to separate from the space was difficult. His new office, although it came to be wonderful in its own way, couldn't have been more different. It felt kind of generic and unremarkable, with the acoustical tile on the ceiling and industrial windows. It had none of the charm inherent in a turn of the century brownstone. But as I said, after a few years that changed for me and although I still missed the view, it actually felt more containing and intimate. He had an amazing collection of things from his life out West, as well as artwork he'd bought and lots of books, so over the course of his time there, he managed to completely transform the space. It felt like I was hanging out in my own house.

JTD **How has your experience with psychoanalysis affected your work, both in *Analysis* and in your practice more broadly?**

ST There are so many things I could say on this topic. One thing that comes to mind is how similar analytic and artistic practices are. In both cases, when they are done well, there is a place where you take everything you know about your craft and put it behind you, giving yourself over to whatever it is you're presented with—you know that all your training and experience will provide the support you need so that you don't have to think about the process. This is certainly what happens to me. After all these years I now know my equipment and the mechanics of making a picture well enough that when I go to photograph something, I don't have to fuss around a lot. I can concentrate on being with the subject matter without the distraction of endlessly calibrating. And I think that's what good analysts do. It takes some confidence, I think, and that confidence comes from training, experience and trusting that you know what you're doing. It's a wonderful place to be, as you know. I've often heard you talk about it when you describe your portrait sessions. Part of what I love about what I do is that, when things are working right, I can lose myself in it for hours. I enter a zone that is free of anxiety and self-consciousness. It's like I lose the edges of myself and merge with whatever is in front of me. I become my subject matter in a way; a kind of mind meld. In some ways, making pictures, when things are really humming along, is a lot like free association.

JTD **Let's talk about the pictures themselves, formally. They're square, color photographs, made on film with your Hasselblad. How did you settle on this approach? Why square, and why color?**

ST I began using a two and a quarter at the Boston Museum School. I suspect it had a lot to do with Diane Arbus, who was a huge influence on all of us who were coming up at that time, and whose signature beyond her subject matter was the use of the square with the black edges of the film showing. I'd been using a 35mm as well, but I associated that more with the documentary photographers of the time—people like Lee Friedlander, Garry Winogrand and Robert Frank. Although I grew to really love their work and was clearly influenced by their style, the kinds of things they were photographing didn't speak to me when I first became aware of them. I had come to photography looking at fashion magazines and my aesthetic was shaped in part by people like Irving Penn, early Richard Avedon, Guy Bourdin and Cecil Beaton. I liked the theatricality of their work. Clearly, my Polaroid portraits were influenced by both Penn and, to a lesser degree, Avedon.

There is also something containing about the square. A horizontal format implies space beyond the frame. A landscape. There is an inherent tension in the square; something slightly claustrophobic about it. Some of my interior work is made in the horizontal but often has a very different feel. I can't imagine the analytic work done in any other format. From the beginning, this work was less about an accurate description of these spaces and more about my subjective experience of them. The square speaks to the sense of containment that is often felt in these offices, the incredible intensity of the therapeutic experience, and the relationship between the patient and the analyst. That being said, I think in most cases they give a fairly accurate sense of what these offices look and feel like. I think shooting them in color was important, in part because so much of what made these spaces intriguing were the analysts' decorative choices. I also wanted the images to convey the sense that these were active working spaces in the present day. I had Edmund Engelman's famous pictures of Freud's consulting room in mind, and wanted to differentiate these images of Engelman's from my own.

JTD Talk to me about your process. When you first walked into one of these offices, how did you respond? Were you looking around, thinking visually about the photograph, or was there a period of time where you'd absorb the energy of the space before getting out your camera? It seems to me that you would have to be open to receiving whatever the space presented to you and respond appropriately with your camera, in order to make pictures that truly resonated, both visually and energetically.

ST I remember my first shoot here in the Boston area. I was acutely aware of the fact that I was taking up people's time and that these analysts were being extremely generous in allowing me into their offices in the first place. So I suspect that initially my approach was a little brusque and no-nonsense. The first analyst I met with seemed a little stunned when I marched into his office and immediately started setting up after briefly introducing myself and giving him a box of prints to look at—he asked me if there wasn't a way we could talk first! I was thrilled, and relaxed immediately. He was lovely and had a lot of interesting things to say about his office and his life. I believe I probably hung out there for a good part of the afternoon. After that, I felt much more comfortable with the process. It was a wonderful couple of years. Analysis attracts interesting, smart and creative people, and I enjoyed having the opportunity to talk with them. Several of them became good friends and remain so to this day. Sadly, some of them are no longer around.

Once I had a few of these shoots under my belt, I often found myself, when I was given the time, standing for a bit before I even brought out my camera, taking it all in. It was much like hanging out in Grand Central Station compared to what I was accustomed to with my other projects, where the emptiness had a spaciousness that was easier in some ways to negotiate and project myself into. That being said, there was always something that stuck out to me in these spaces that begged to be focused on. I knew almost as soon as I stepped in the door how I wanted to record the office. In some cases, I had a limited amount of time to photograph, so the process, by necessity, became more compressed. I had to take everything in fairly quickly, set up and start working immediately. When I had the luxury of time, I would still have one favorite shot that spoke to me, but I would also sit with the space for a while to discover other angles or details that I wanted to capture.

JTD I'm interested in the idea of loss and the emptiness left in its wake. Loss is an interesting and complicated experience that can lead to all kinds of things—sadness, mourning, seeking, healing, rebuilding, redefining oneself, renegotiating one's place in the world... Obviously, losing your mother at an early age affected everything about the trajectory of your life and work.

ST You're right, my mom dying was life-altering. It's hard to know how it would have been different if she hadn't died, but I do know that it absolutely affected the direction my work took. I have to wonder if I wouldn't have pursued something in the applied arts, like design or fashion... or becoming a detective. Of course, as I talked about earlier, I wasn't really on any kind of track artistically. I was still quite young. But the direction I ended up taking, both with the family/portrait work and the interior work, was absolutely driven by a need to process what had happened to me and my family.

Interestingly and sadly, I relived the experience of losing my mother when my therapist became ill with a serious and debilitating form of cancer. Much like with my mother, I had a hard time facing the fact that he would probably die from this. As his cancer started to overtake him, he grew thinner, but continued to work and I realized at some point that when he turned to the side, I would look away. From the front, it wasn't so obvious how much weight he had lost. It's pretty clear to me now that it felt too much like watching my mother disappear. The bottom line is that there is no processing something like this at the ages my brothers and I were when she went. I think when you're young you internalize these losses, which then sets you up as you move into the future to see everything in your life in terms of loss. Since you are still growing and developing, the loss becomes a part of your DNA. When you're older, you experience it in a different way. You've had a chance to come into yourself and form relationships and understand death differently. The death of a parent when you're young is a kind of blunt force trauma. Since one has a certain resiliency that comes with being younger, you recover, but it can have lasting scars that get papered over as you grow up. Sometimes these scars don't appear until later, when you begin to lose the people in your life in a more age-appropriate way. Experiencing death is hard no matter what age you are, but maybe it's made more difficult as you get older because every death resonates with this pivotal early loss.

JTD **Right, that makes sense. In relation to your pictures, I'm thinking about the relationship of loss to the healing that can follow in a psycho-analyst's office. How do you think about the interplay between loss and healing, between sadness and rebirth? Did you feel this complicated, multilayered energy in these spaces? What do you think ultimately happens to this buildup of energy?**

ST I was thinking the other day, as I came back from a friend's memorial, that there is no way we can get through life without feeling the pain of loss unless we lock ourselves up and never allow ourselves to feel love. There is no growth or healing without it. I'm not talking about large-scale catastrophic loss, through genocide, for example, or brought on by massive natural disasters like earthquakes, but the day-to-day, year-to-year kind of losses that we inevitably experience as we get on in life. I'm not sure that the process is all that linear. I think we move through our lives dealing with whatever gets thrown our way, often circling back and re-experiencing the same thing over and over only with a slightly different perspective each time. I remember thinking at one point, maybe a few years into my work with my thera-pist, that nothing seemed to be changing. It felt like I was repeatedly going over the same terrain. But then one day I realized that my life had changed in significant ways, only it had happened so incrementally that I hadn't even noticed. It wasn't an ah-ha! thing. It was more like a slow dawning. So the word 'rebirth' is a little misleading unless you think about the gestation period in terms of decades. I also think the process is ongoing, and often continues long after you've left therapy. Even though my therapist is no longer here, the work we did continues to resonate and build on itself, not unlike the process of making work. Each project builds on the one before it.

But getting back to the analytic spaces... one of the things I found interesting about these offices was the sense of tranquility and containment that I felt in most of them. I know what it's like to walk into a space and immediately feel uncomfortable, like I'm picking up on something a little unhinged. Considering the fact that one rarely goes to a therapist just to shoot the breeze, it would make sense that the energy in these offices might feel a little jagged, but that wasn't the case. Some of the therapists whose offices I photographed had either fled Europe during the rise of Hitler and the Nazis, or had been sent to the camps and survived, or had family and friends who died there. So they were undoubtedly bringing their own acutely felt sense of trauma and dislocation to their work. Gela Rosenthal, the analyst in Buenos Aires who got me started on this project, left Europe in 1938, most likely to escape the Nazis. I realized as I sat in her office reading one day that she had experienced both the Jewish diaspora and the trauma of the Dirty War in Argentina. Gela told me that her husband was imprisoned by the military dictatorship at that time. One night, a prison guard arrived at her door. Apparently, she had helped his brother some years before and, out of gratitude, he told her where she could find her husband. Her history, along with the histories of the hundreds of patients she had seen over the course of her practice, were embedded in her office... a lovely, light-filled space that remained discreet and betrayed none of the stories and confidences, difficulties and joys that Gela and her patients had brought to it over the course of her time there. It occurs to me that in some sense these offices are places where trauma is turned into something manageable—that what I felt in these spaces was a protected containment that made transformation and healing possible.

I have no doubt that every space has an energetic presence—sometimes strong, other times not so much—and I don't think that this buildup of energy is limited to constructed space. When I was out in Wyoming at the Ucross Foundation, I was struck by how sentient and alive the landscape was. I was initially leery of spending time out there because I'm more comfortable in a contained landscape. My house is surrounded by trees and very shaded. I grew up in New England and feel protected here. When I first got off the plane in Wyoming, I felt like I had landed on Mars—nothing but landscape for as far as the eye could see. After settling in, the first thing I did was hop in my rental car and start driving. Every now and then, I would drive through an area that shook me to the core. I would have to pull the car over to catch my breath. Someone I mentioned this to suggested that I might have driven through a Native American burial site. I was also haunted by the sudden and frequent appearances of strip mining operations—hills with their tops sheared off, the earth exposed and raw. I'm also reminded of a trip I took to Gettysburg with my brother and sister-in-law some years back. It was a chilly, gray, drizzly day and the landscape sat quietly in front of us, betraying none of the horror that had been perpetrated upon its verdant and gently rolling fields. But it definitely gave off a palpable feeling of something unsettled and sad.

JTD **Right. It's interesting to think of the energy held in spaces themselves, and how that energy may or may not overlap with what we are individually going through at the specific point in time in which we experience them—whether we are able to receive it or not, whether we are tuned in to the correct wavelength.**

What was the response within the analytic community to this work, both while you were making it and also once it was out in the world as photographs? Were analysts generally interested in having their spaces photographed, or did you encounter certain privacy con-cerns, or a reluctance to make these highly personal spaces more public? How did the analysts participating in the project respond to your photographs of their offices?

ST It was interesting. I got no resistance down in Buenos Aires but Gela was setting up these appointments for me, so I don't really know whether anyone said no to her. In most cases, I never even met the ana-lysts when I went in to photograph their offices. They would arrange with a housekeeper to let me in while they were out doing errands. When I got back to the States, it was different. There are four analytic organizations that I worked with in the Boston area, including the Jungian Institute. I initially got my start with analysts that I met through The Massachusetts Institute of Psychoanalysis (MIP). Through them I gained access to the Boston Psychoanalytic Society and Institute (BPSI). Once I got the mailing lists for these organizations, I sent out a letter describing what I was doing and asking their members if they would like to participate. The reactions were varied. Many were absolutely amenable to it. Some were supportive of the project but didn't feel comfortable having me photograph their spaces out of concern for their patients' privacy and possibly for their own as well. And then there were a few who I sensed were deeply skeptical of the project and my reasons for doing it. All in all, I found the community to be very generous and supportive. In many cases, I wouldn't photograph but would have lengthy conversations with analysts on the phone. I believe that, for the most part, the people I worked with liked having pictures of their offices.

JTD **Where does this body of work sit in relation to your other work? What have you worked on previously that may have influenced or informed it, and what has followed, or is yet to come?**

ST The analytic images seem slightly separate from my other work because they aren't really dealing with loss in a direct way. I see this body of work more as a contemplation on human connection and the energy and potential healing these relationships generate, as seen in the configuration of furniture and the objects that the analysts choose to place in their spaces. As I mentioned before, it was, in part, the reason why I initially had a hard time knowing how to approach these offices. They were full of life—present and past—and almost felt too crowded to approach with a camera. They were buzzing with a free-floating energy that was palpable and hard to identify.

My earlier work, like the abandoned homes in North Carolina and the pictures I took of my relatives' houses after they passed or, more recently, the Phantom Limb project, were clearly made in an attempt to come to terms with this early childhood loss. The Phantom Limb work centered around my mother's house in New Hampshire, which my brothers and I still have. It came together shortly after my brother Geof died suddenly, so it started off as one thing and very quickly became about losing him.

The North Carolina work especially resonated with me. Somewhere in the middle of that project I realized that these structures were physical embodiments of the Mother. Most of them were farmhouses as opposed to large plantation homes. They were homes that had raised families and witnessed generations of people come into the world and leave it. They had a nurturing quality about them. I found myself relating to them in a very specific way: as one middle-aged female body to another. The Boston Athenaeum also felt very corporeal to me. I had only known it when it was packed with books but once it was emptied out in preparation for demolition, it felt very fragile and ethereal... much like a cathedral. Again, there was a way that I could relate to it as another body... granted, a very large body, nothing like the farmhouses, but a body nonetheless. I actually got quite protective of it and dreaded its impending destruction once the renovation began.

It's funny though. I also see the analytic images stemming directly from the first interiors I made out in Indiana in the 70's—the pictures of my grandmother's house. Furniture as a stand in for the human body features strongly in both. I have a picture of my grandfather's chair that feels structurally identical to an image I took down in Buenos Aires of a large, old fashioned, over-stuffed plush analyst's chair. I sometimes put them together in the beginning of the line-up when I exhibit this body of work.

At this point, I'm concentrating on pulling together work that has never been seen, specifically the work centered around my family. I've been documenting my family and friends from the very beginning and would like to pull that body of work together in a more formal way, ideally as a book. I came to photography through the printed page and that's where I'd like to bring it back to. I love books, and have been an avid collector of art books for most of my life. I see them as portable exhibitions that don't depend upon a physical space, that can be viewed intimately and whenever you want to. My books may be the last things to go if and when I finally have to move out of my house—the books and the artwork.

Newtonville, MA
Blue couch with multiple portrait of Freud, 2000

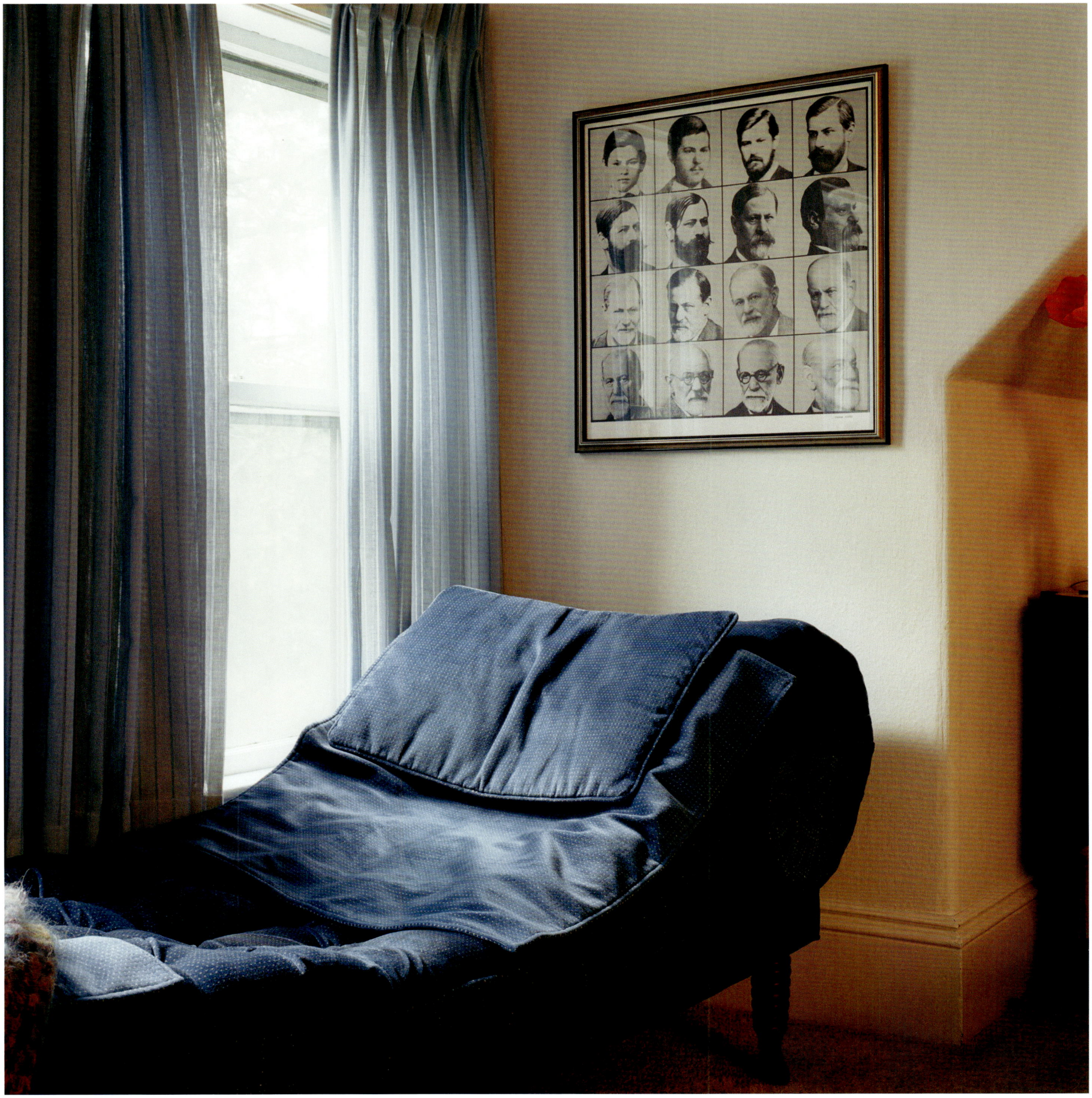

Providence, RI
Patient's chair with three-headed lamp, 2000

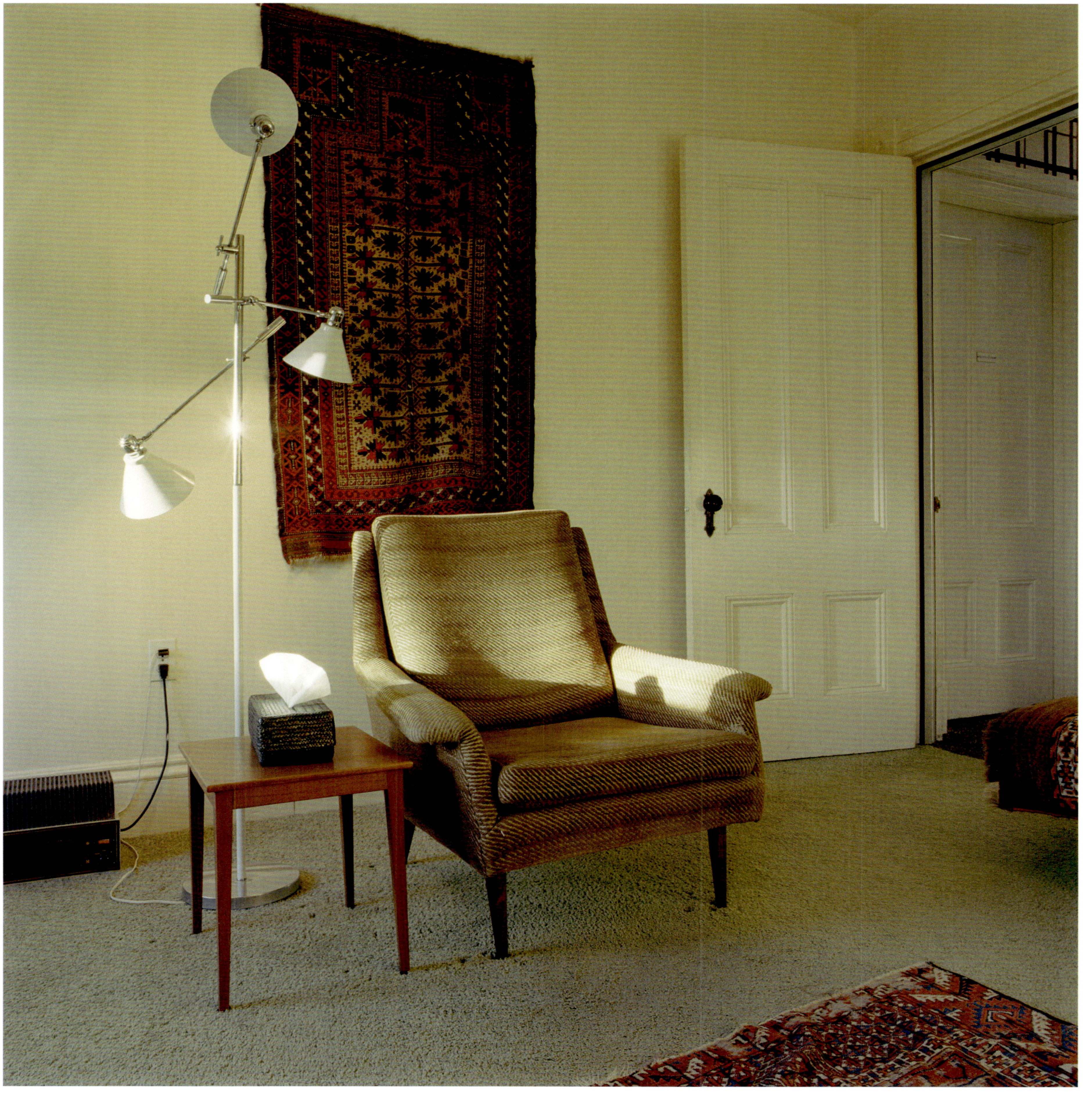

Buenos Aires

Office with beige leather couch and pillows, 1999

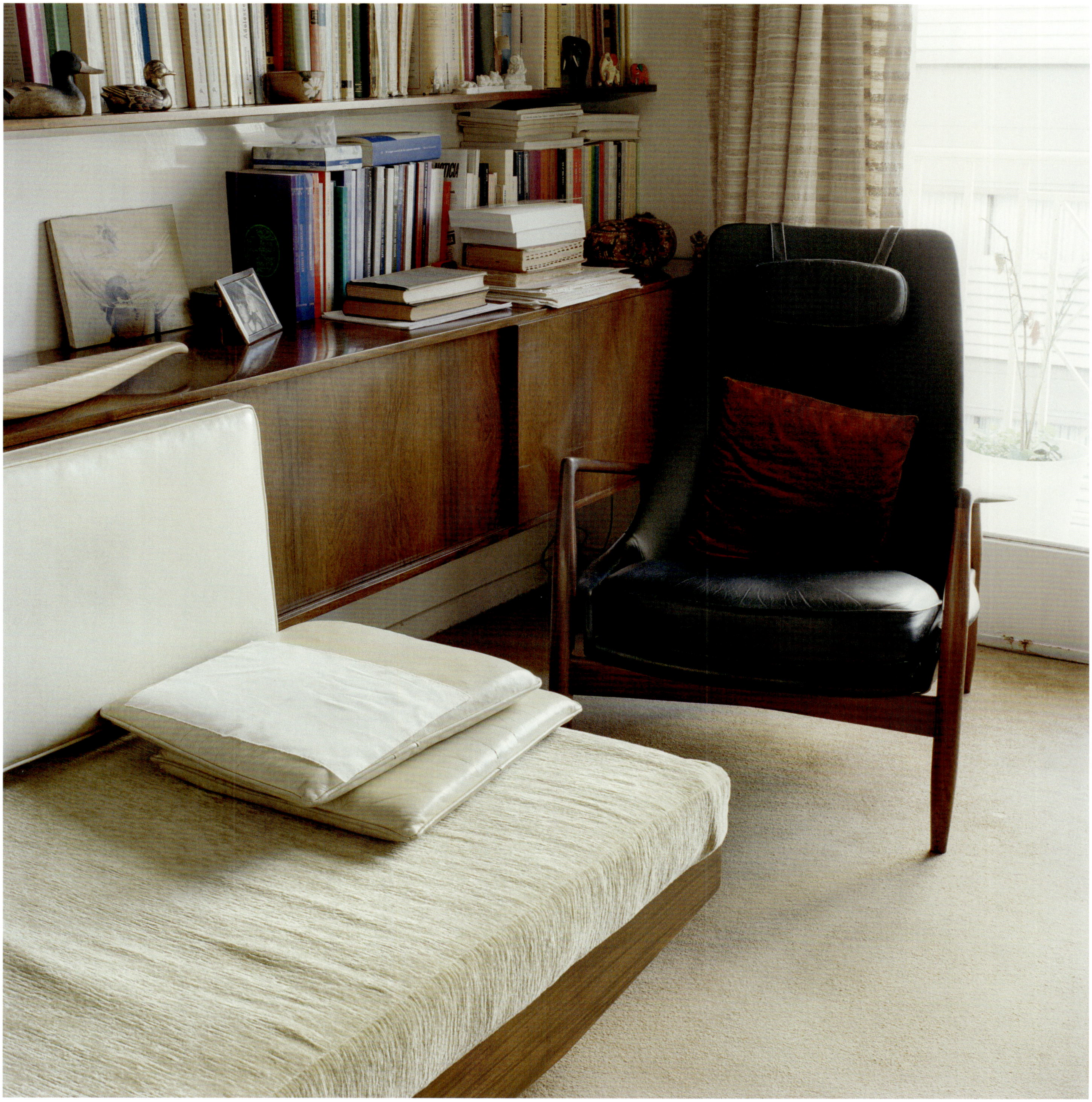

Lexington, MA
Analyst's office with toy box and two chairs, 2000

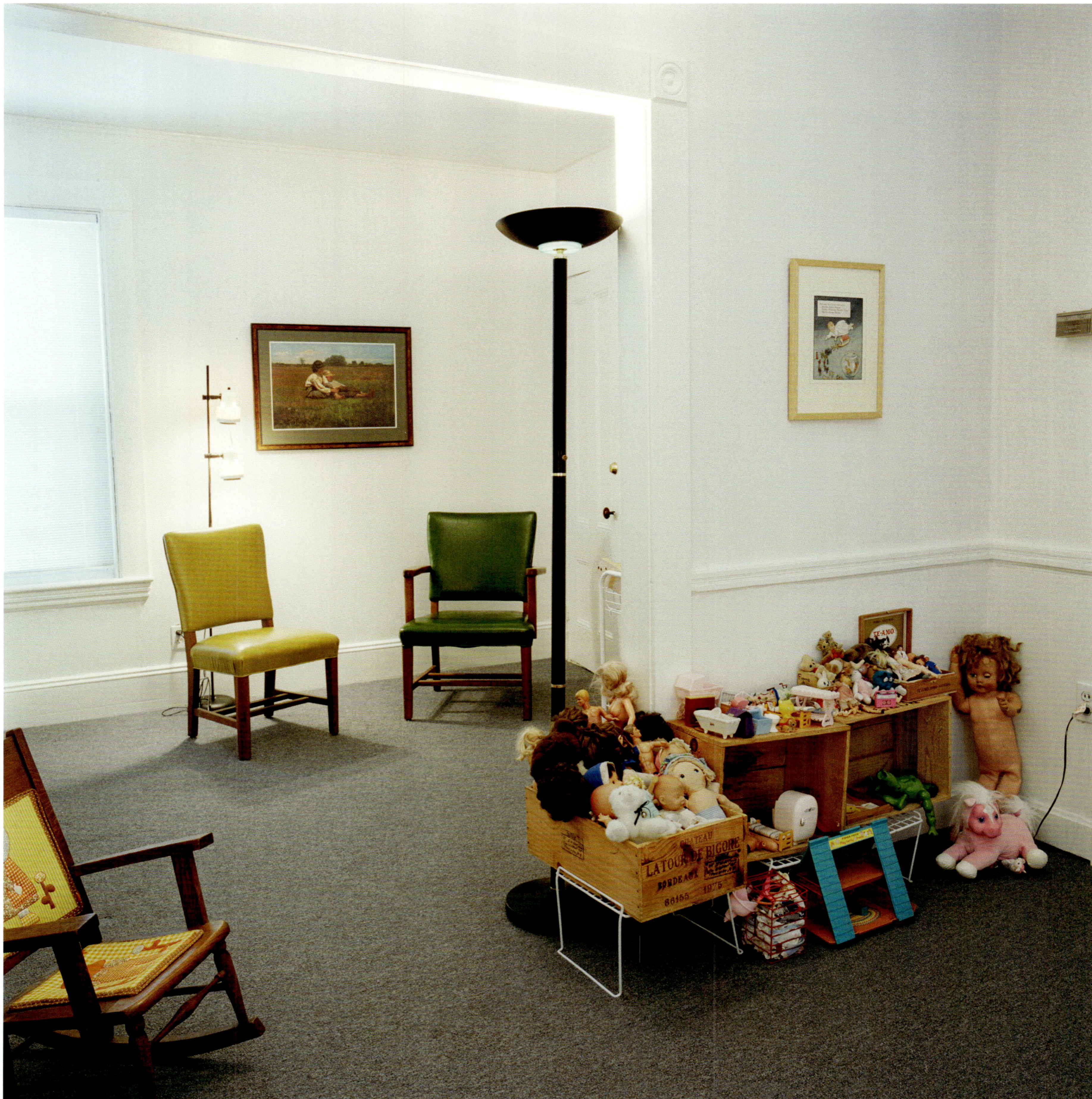

Cambridge, MA
Office with couch under bookshelves, 2000

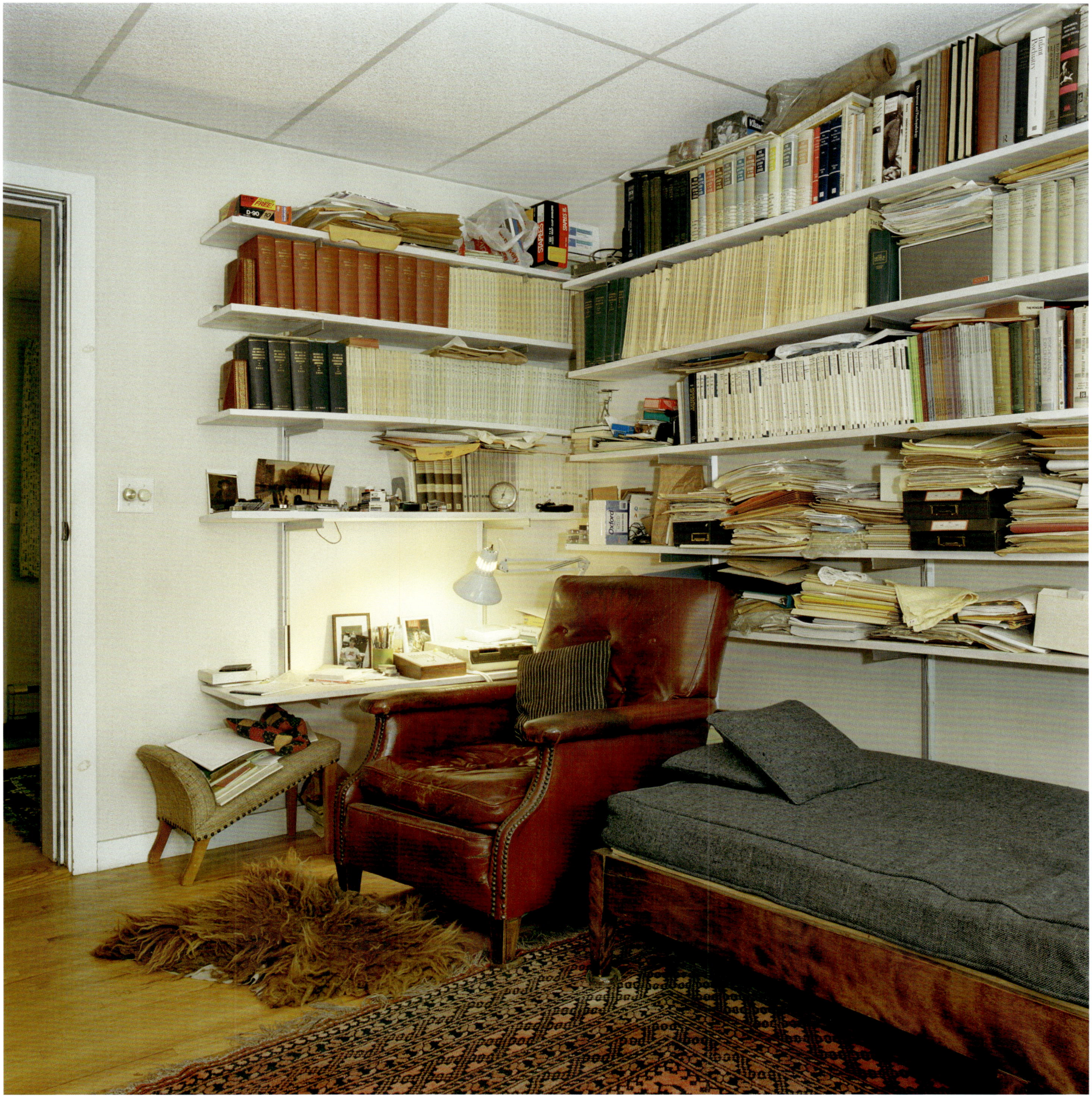
FREE
D-90
STAPLES
Oxford

Cambridge, MA
Attic office with brown leather couch and decorative pillow, 2000

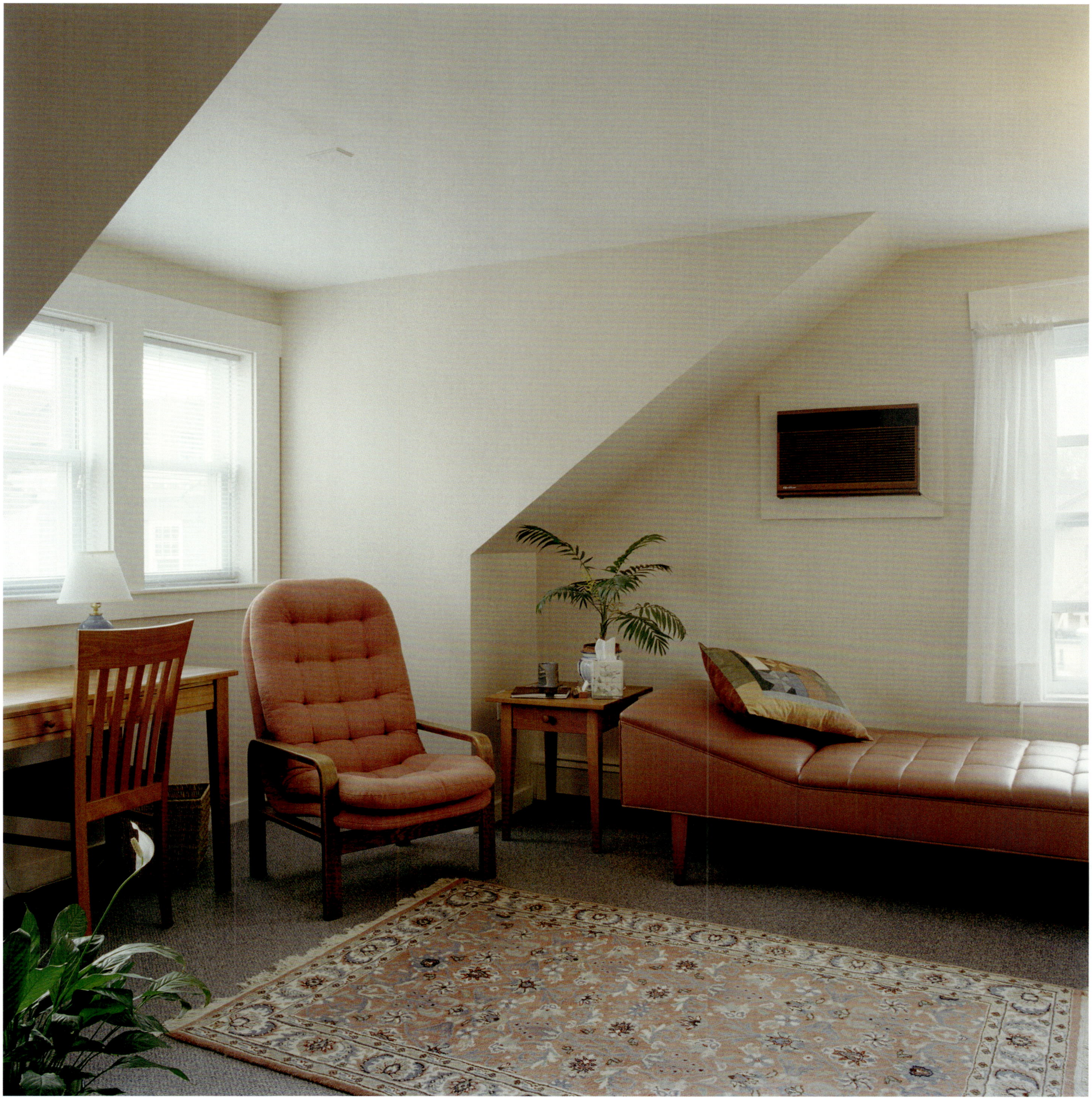

Jamaica Plain, MA
Analyst's chair with Corinthian capital side table, 2000

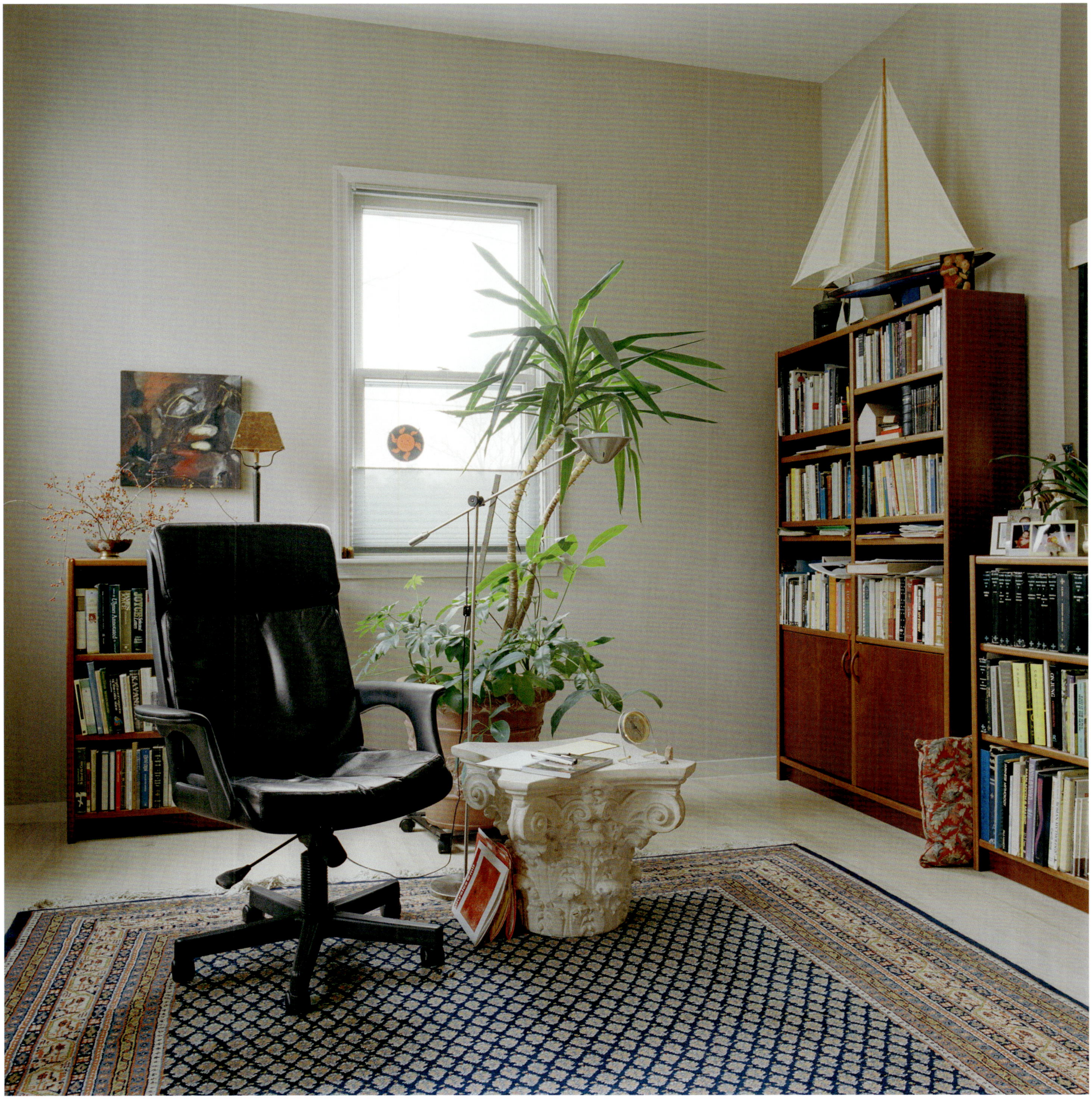

Belmont, MA
Office with rocking chair and brown fabric couch, 2000

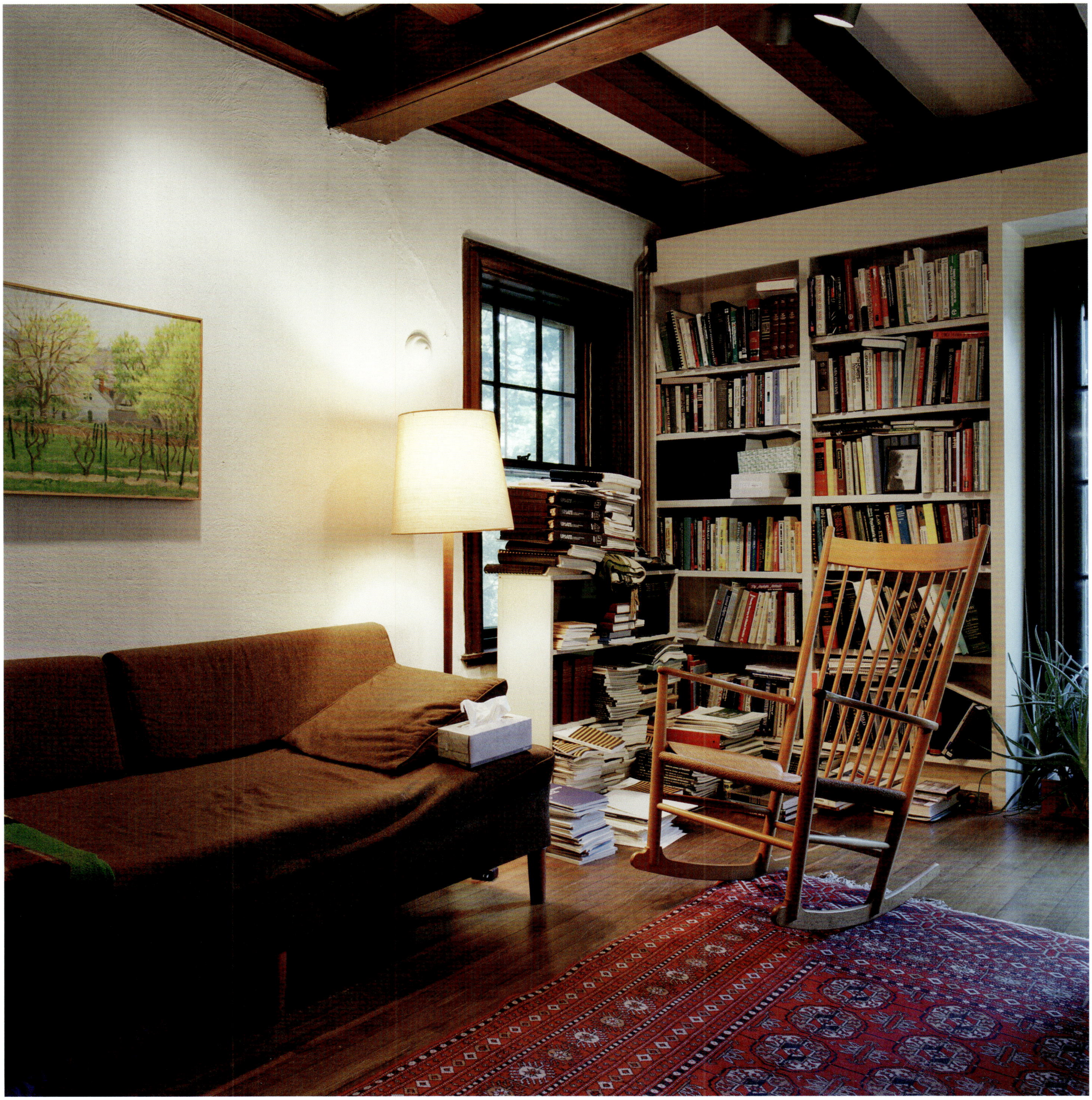

Cambridge, MA
Office with green leather analyst's chair and three-legged table lamp, 2000

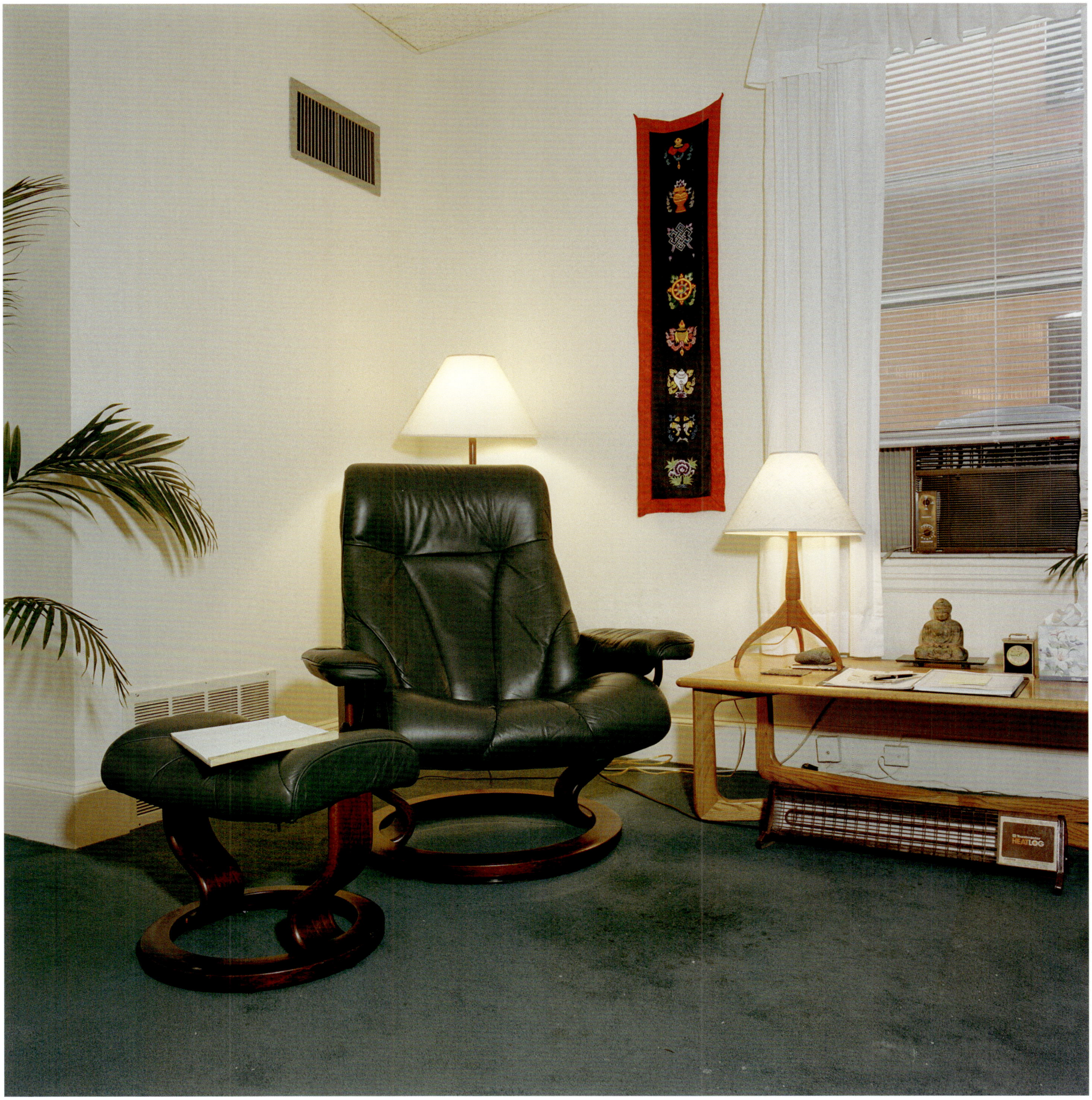
HEATLOG

Buenos Aires
Wood-paneled office with floor-to-ceiling windows, 1999

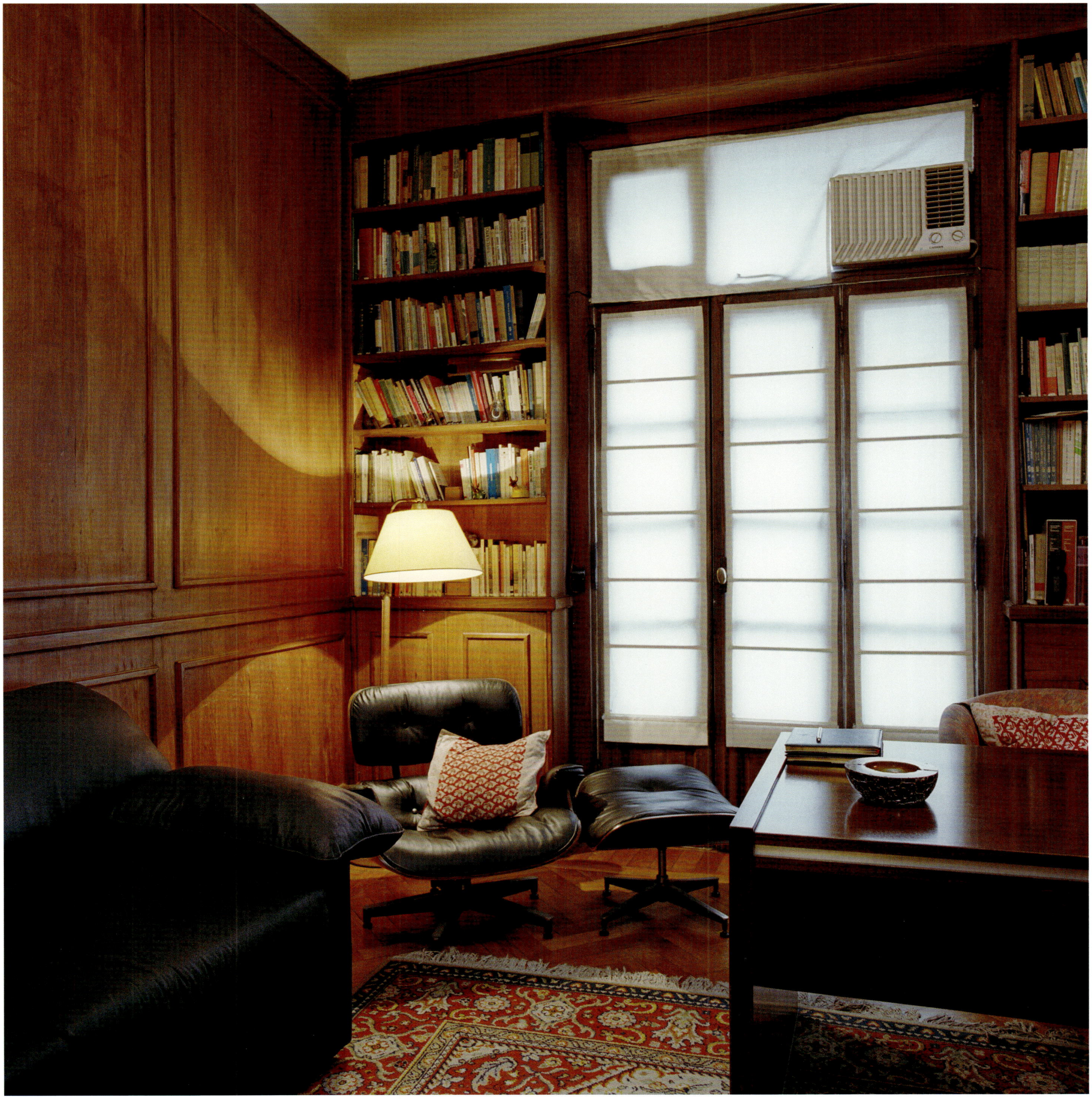

Andover, MA
Office with chartreuse analyst's chair and brown floral print, 2000

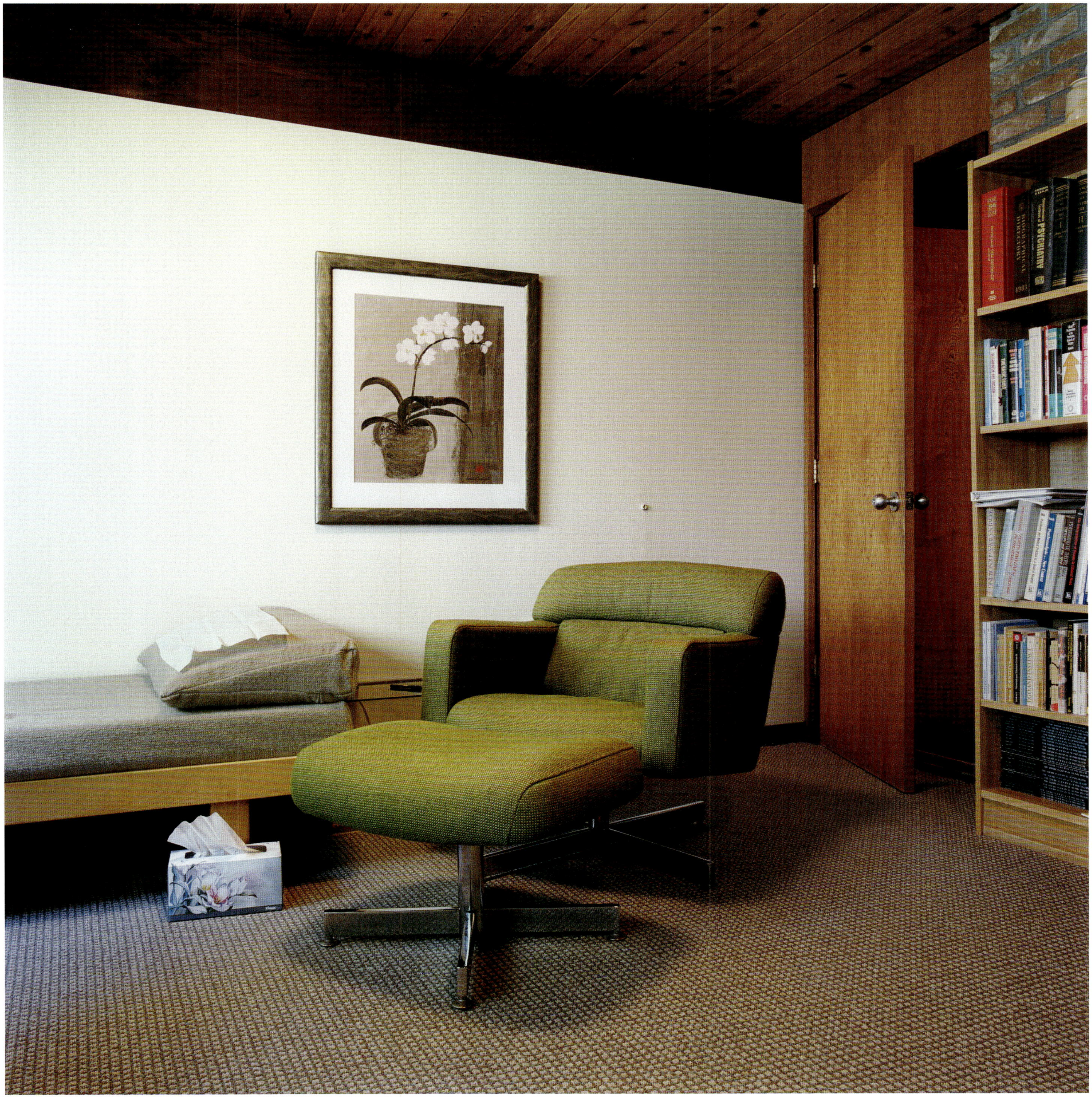

Buenos Aires
Office with wall-mounted television and picture of Freud, 1999

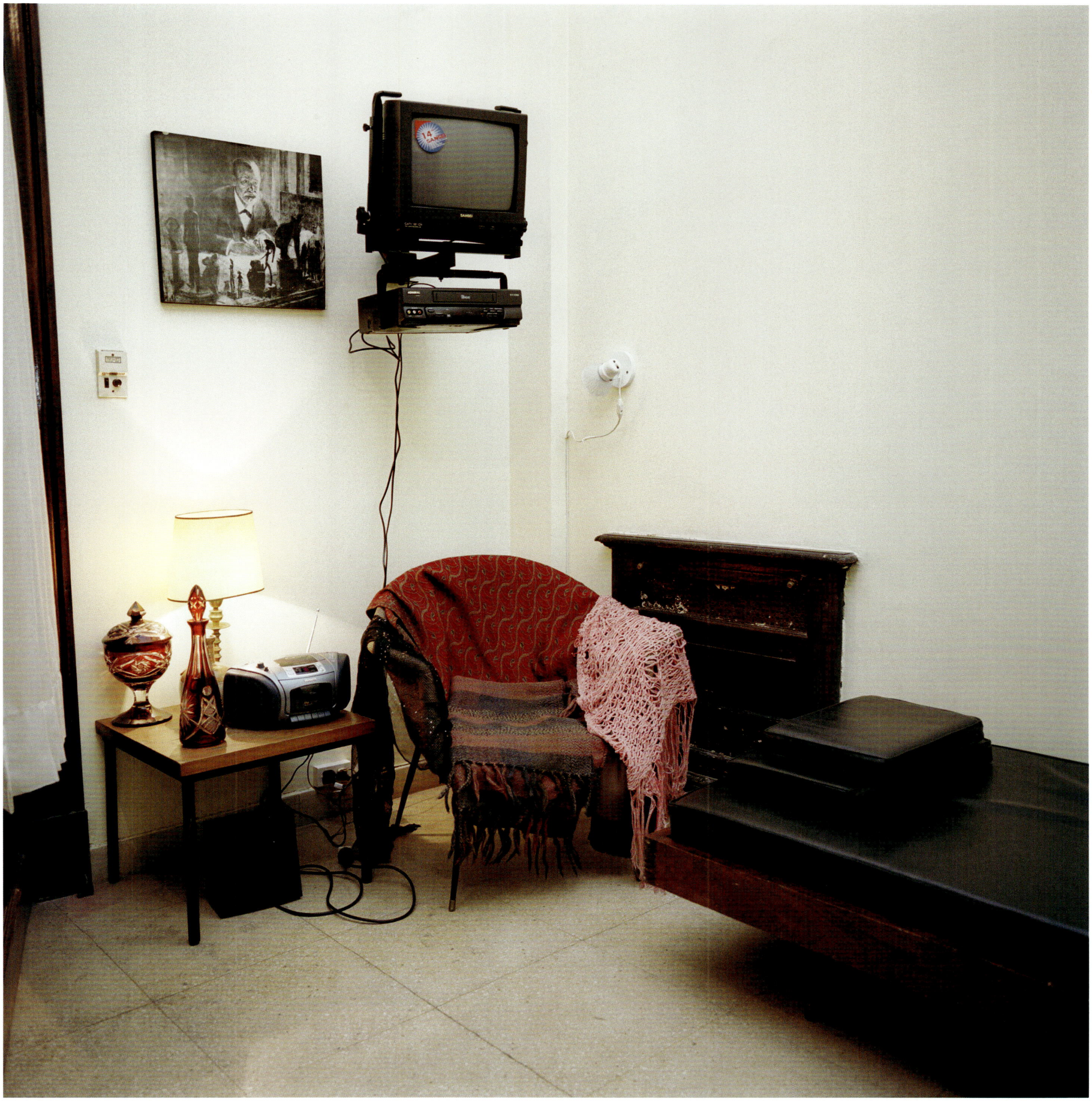

Belmont, MA

Attic office with ochre analyst's chair and deep red fabric couch, 2000

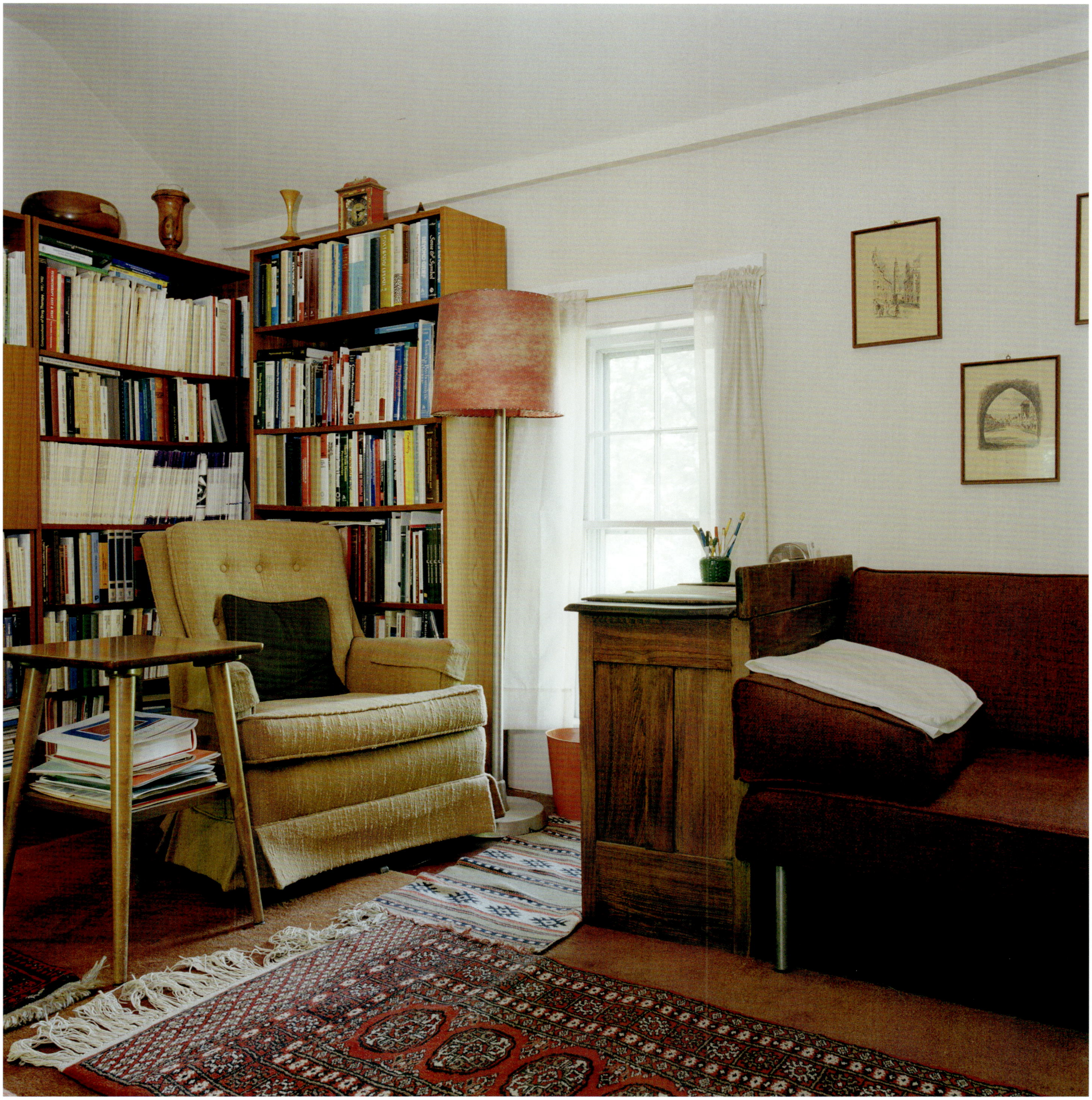

Lexington, MA
Office with blue couch and Botello wall print, 2000

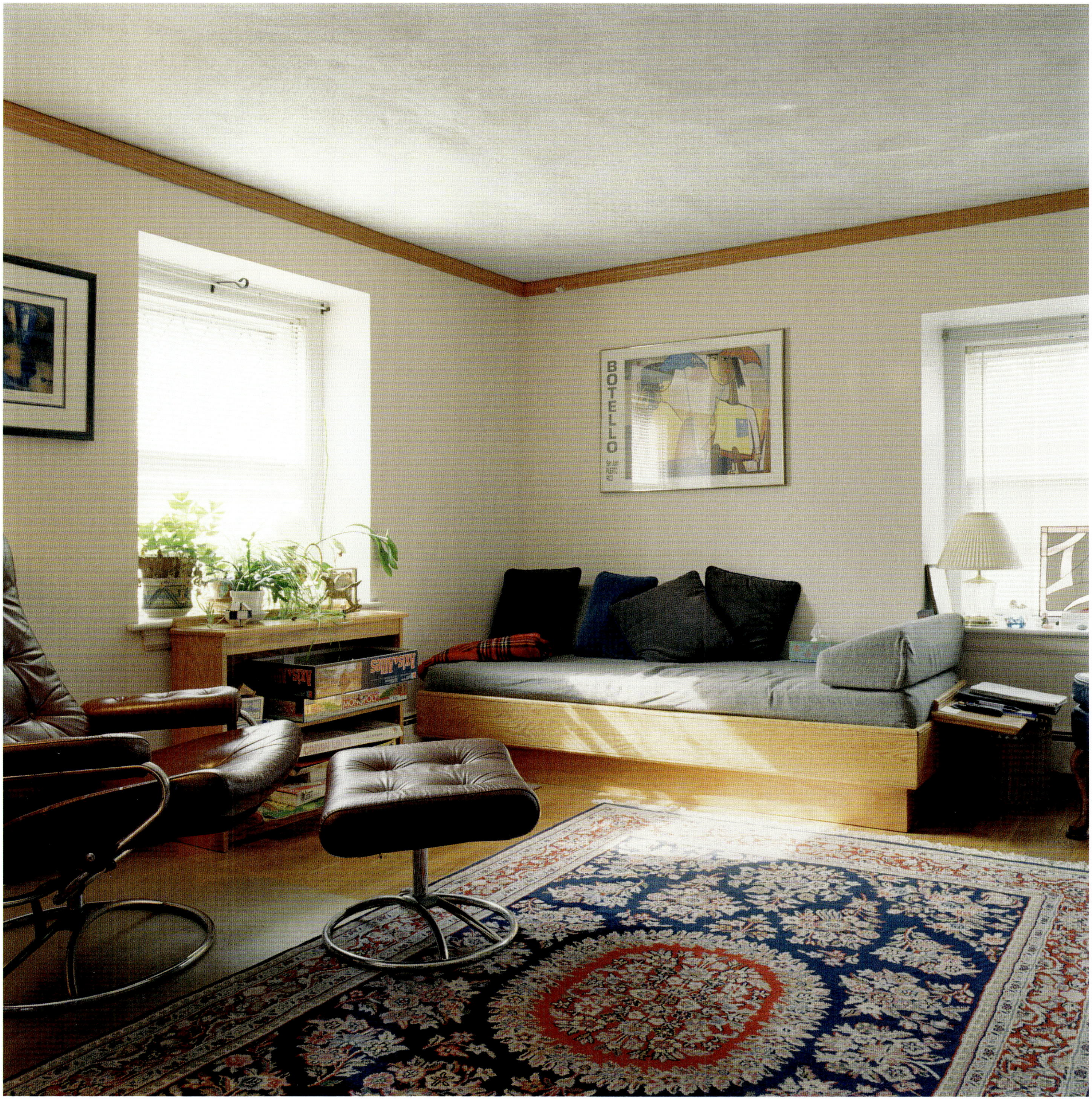
BOTELLO

Brookline, MA
Office with blue couch, stucco walls and African mask, 2000

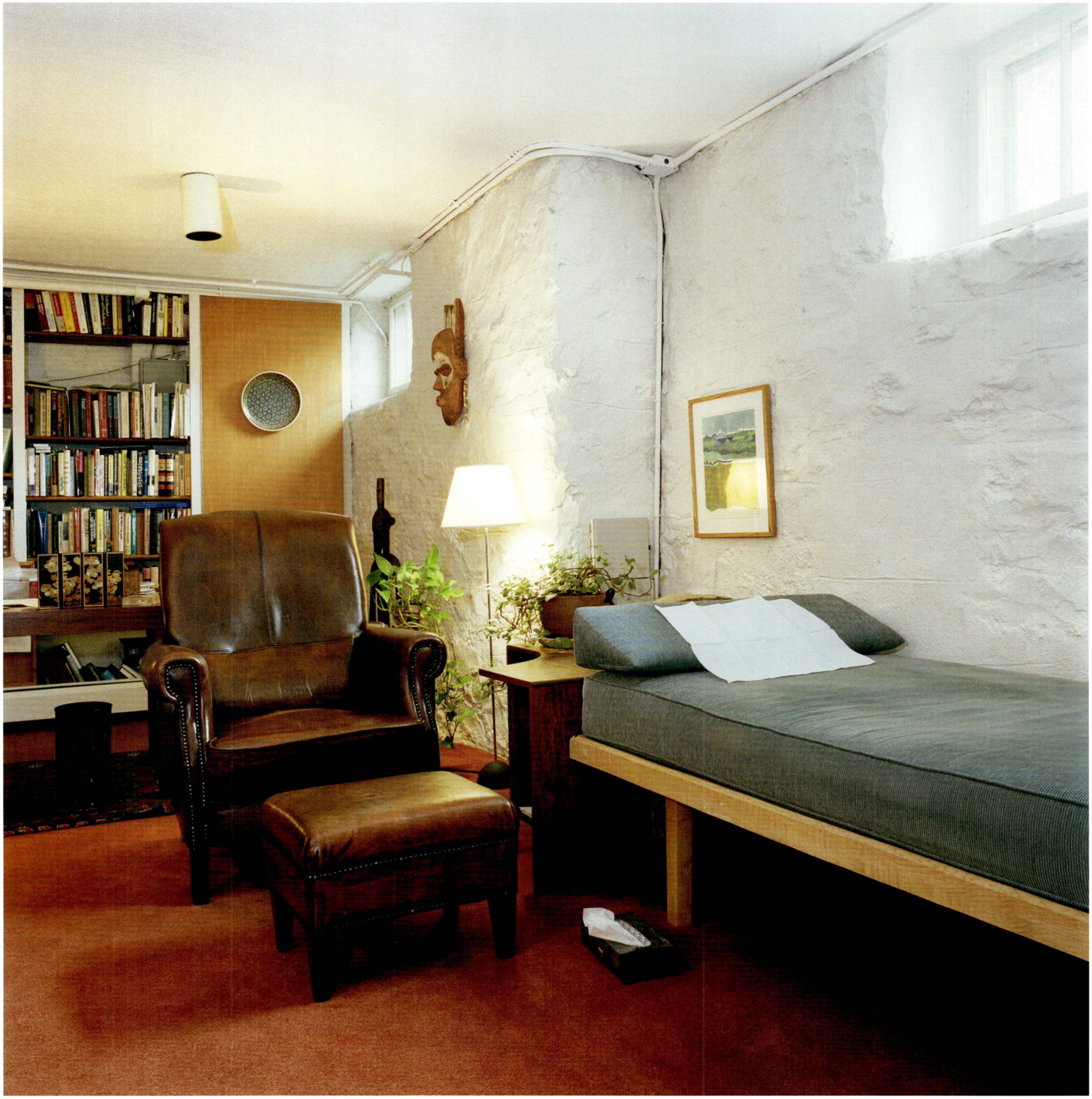

Brookline, MA
Analyst's chair with worn leather hassock, 2000

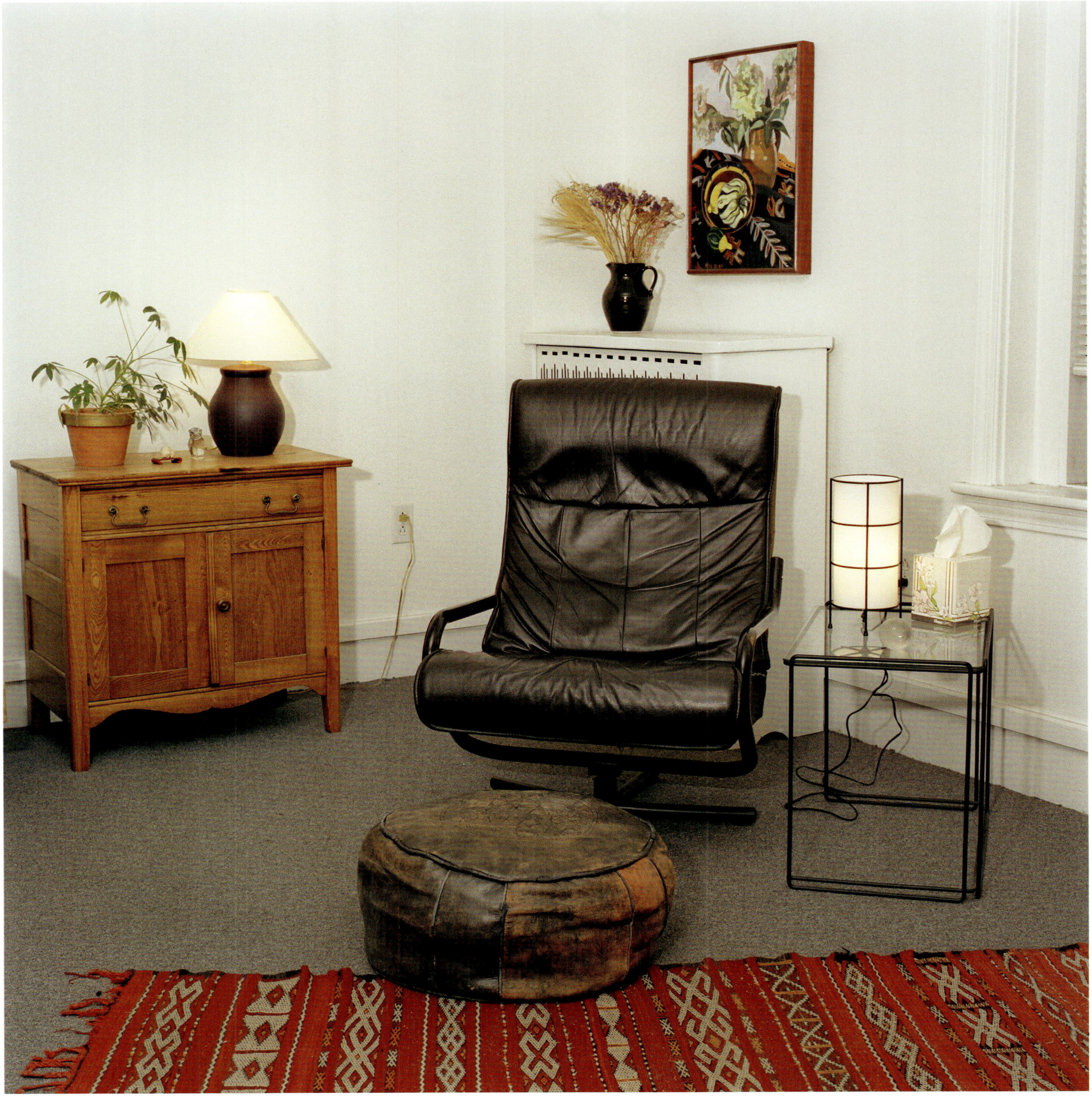

Framingham, MA
Analyst's office with memo-covered wall, 2000

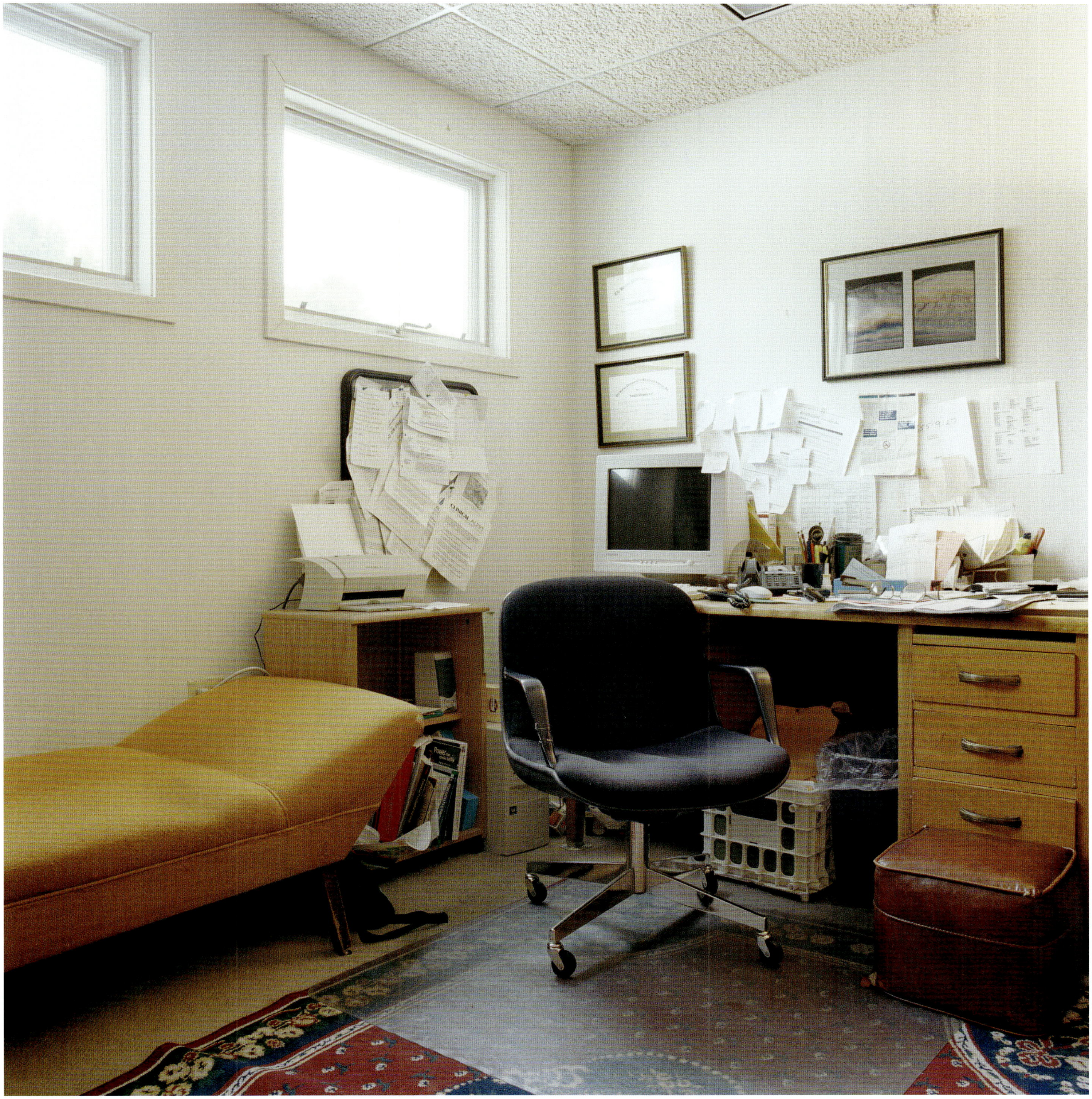
CLINICAL ALERT

Brookline, MA
Patient's chair with vase of red tulips, 2000

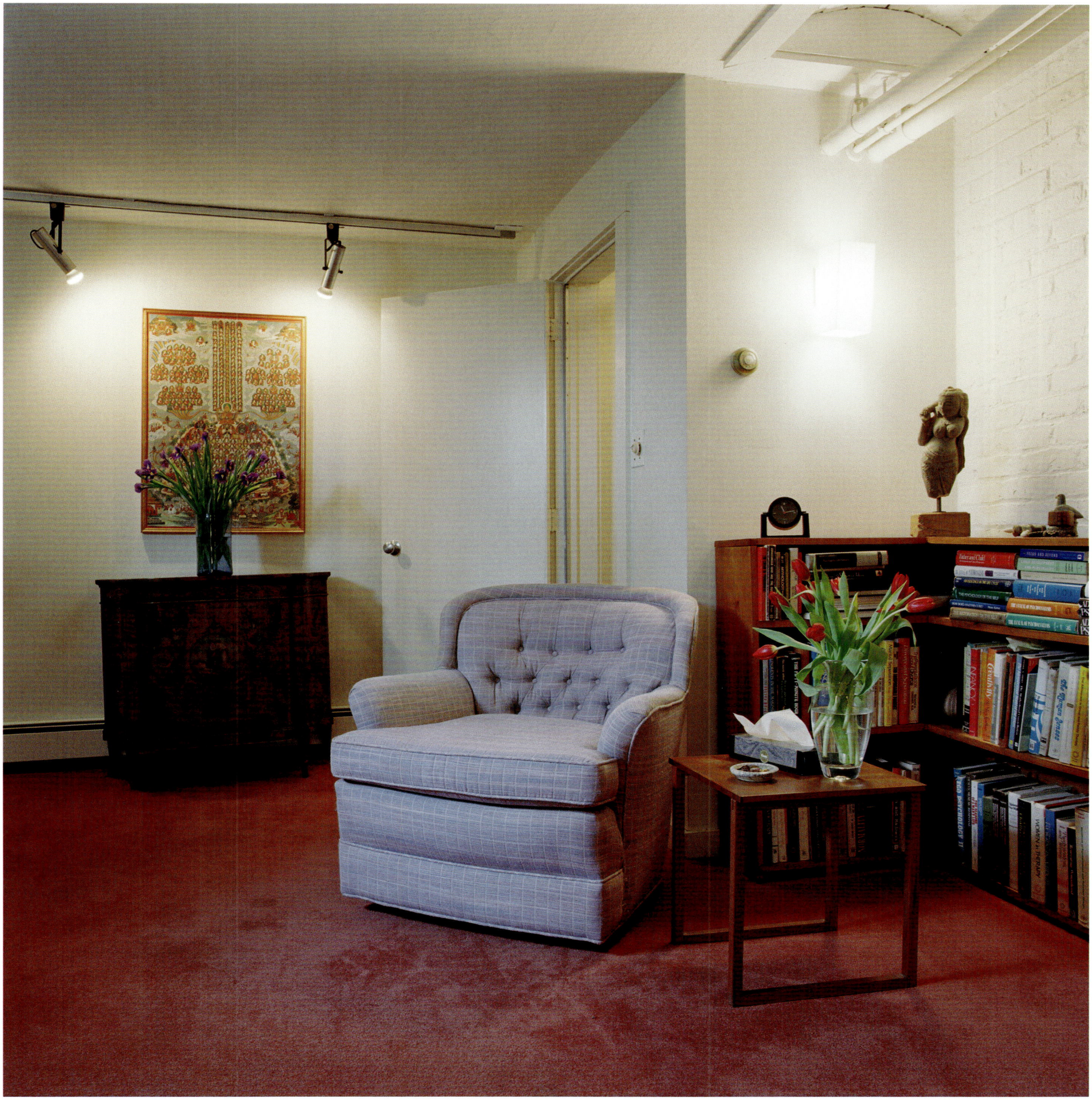
Father and Child
FREUD AND BEYOND
THE PSYCHOLOGY OF THE SELF
INFANCY
Creativity
EGO PSYCHOLOGY II
WOMEN IN THERAPY

Chestnut Hill, MA
Office with beige tweed fabric couch, 2000

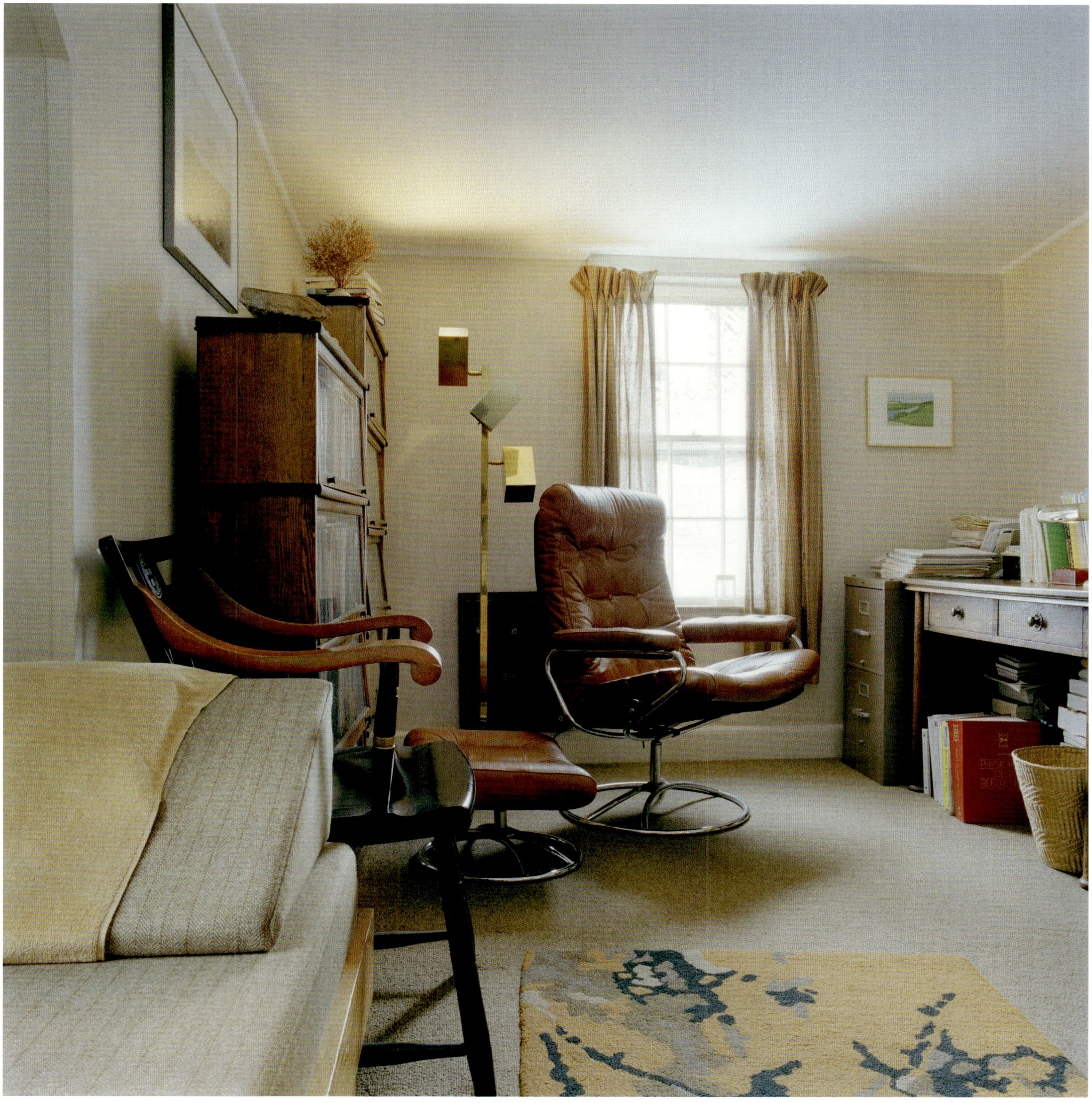

Brookline, MA
Office with striped fabric couch and plaid pillow, 2000

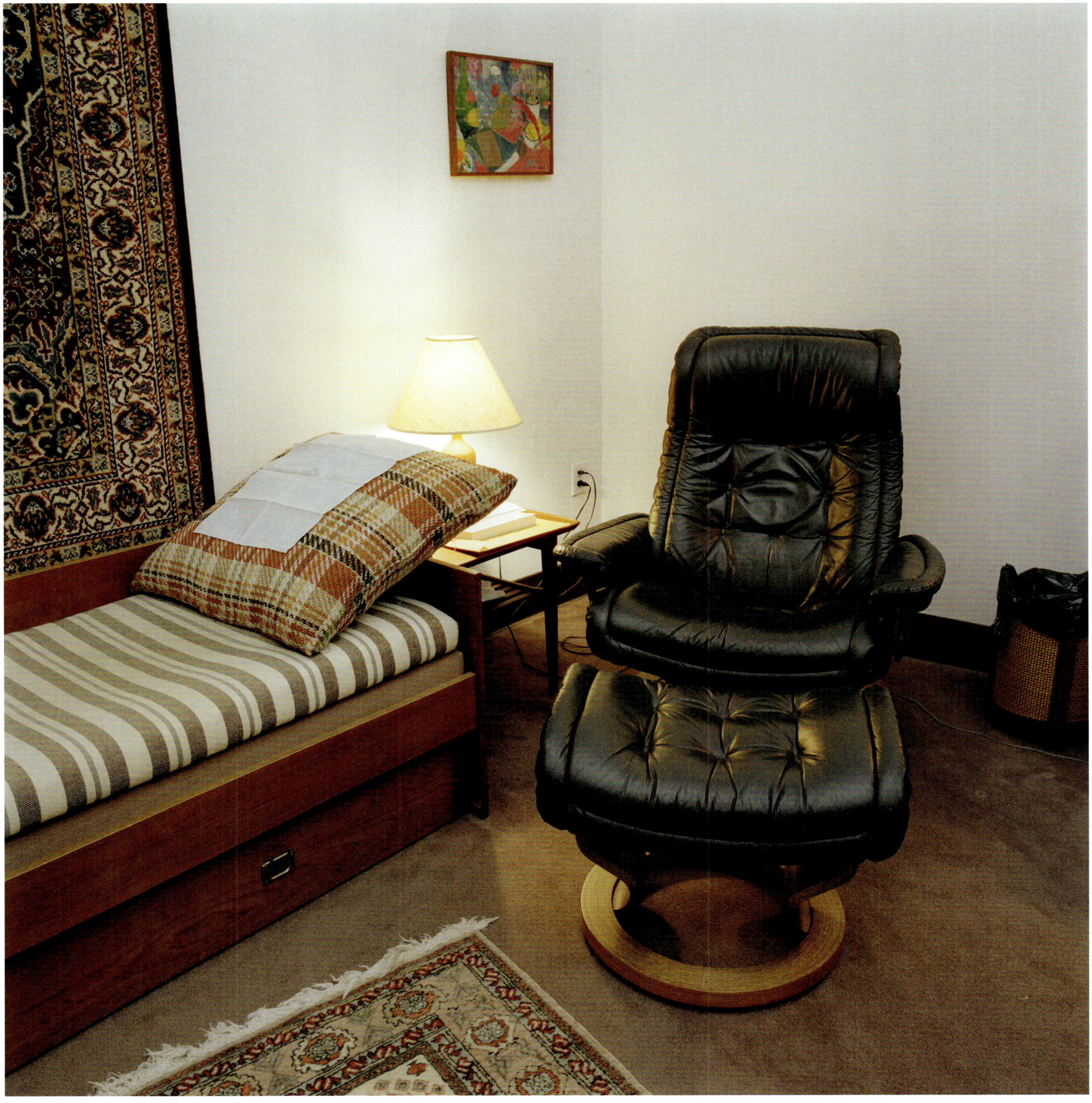

Providence, RI
Yellow office with brown leather couch and rocking chair, 2000

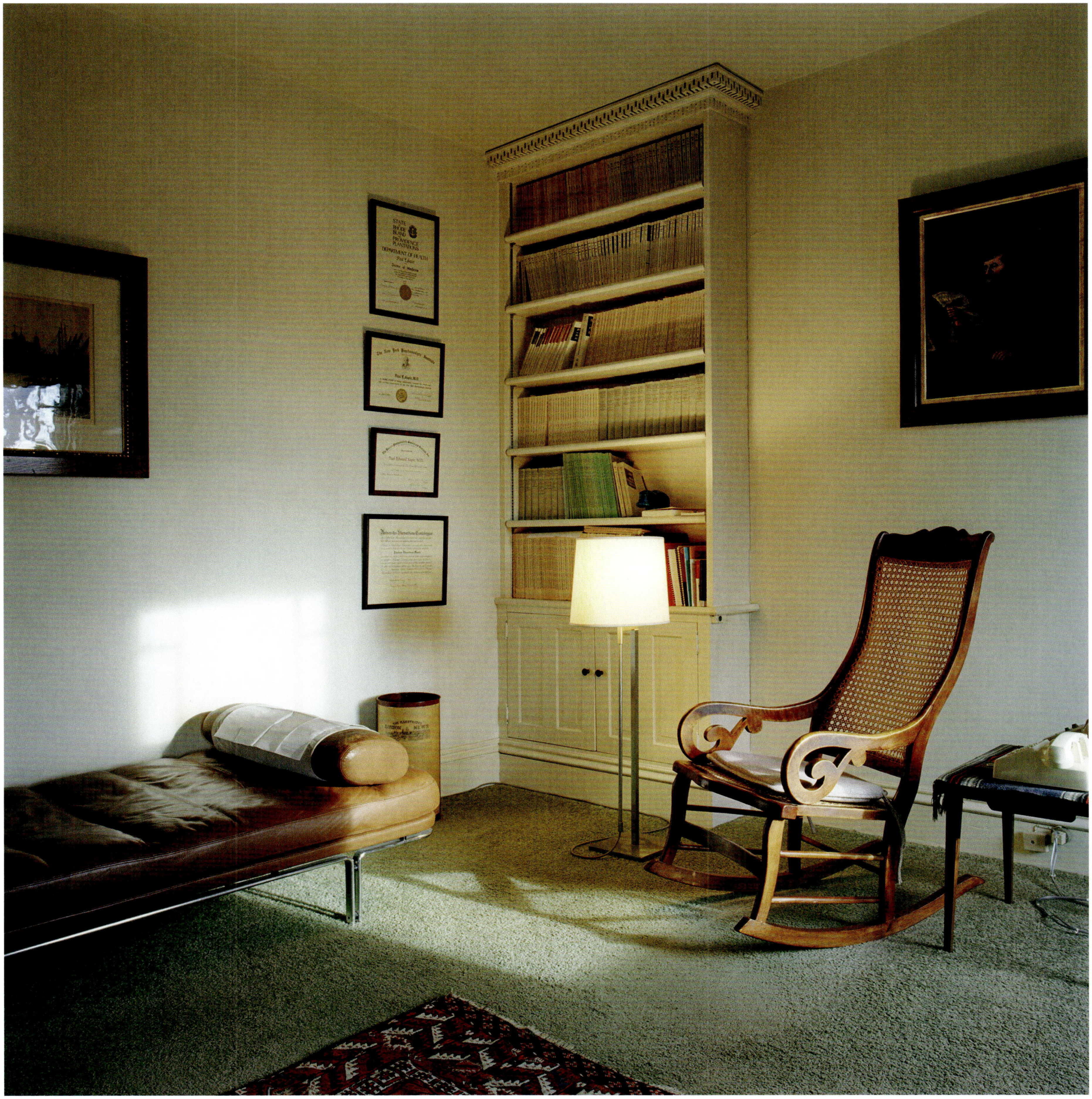

Cambridge, MA
Office with black leather couch and bentwood chair, 2000

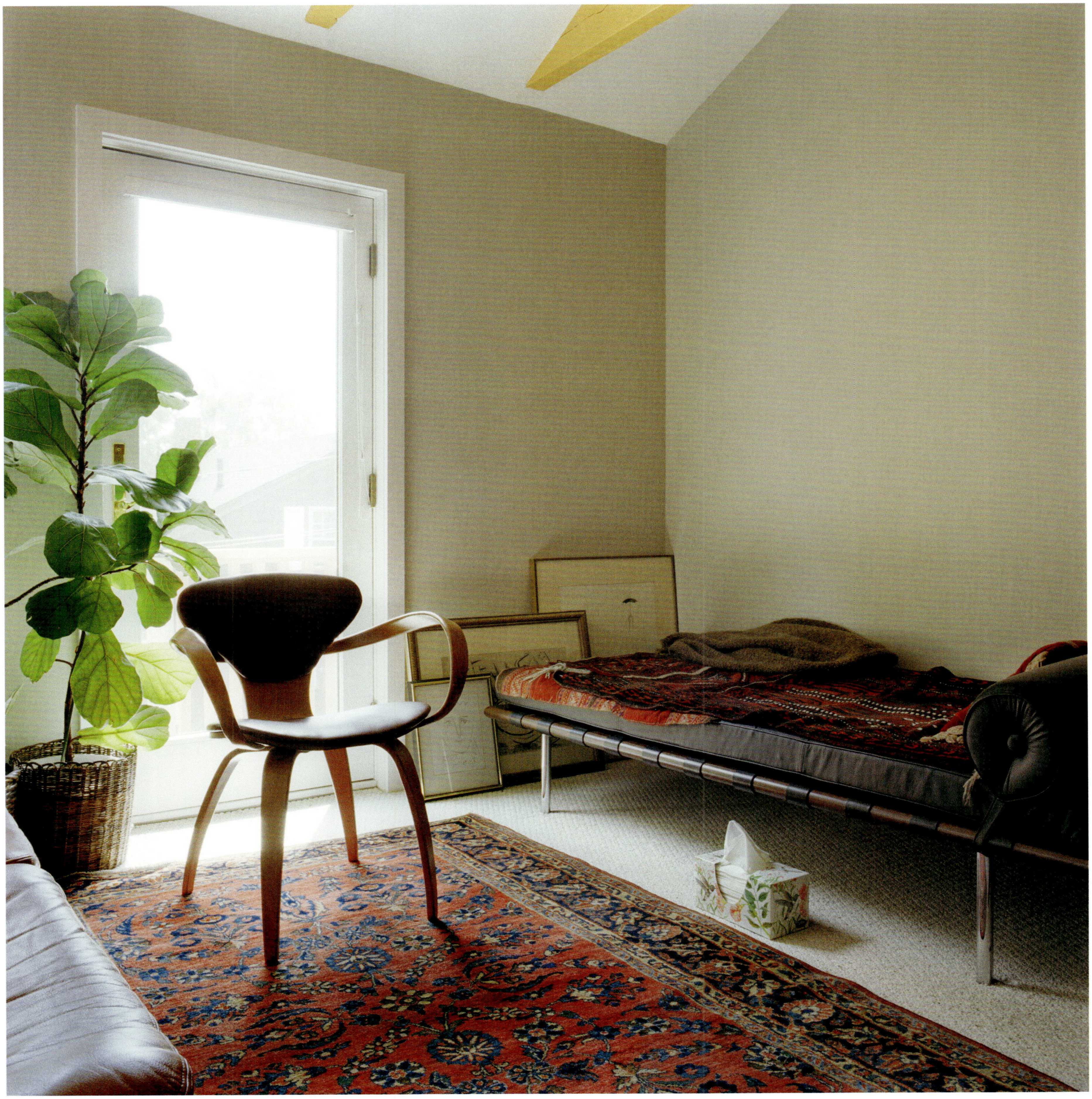

Boston, MA

Patient's chair with yellow ceramic lamp, 2000

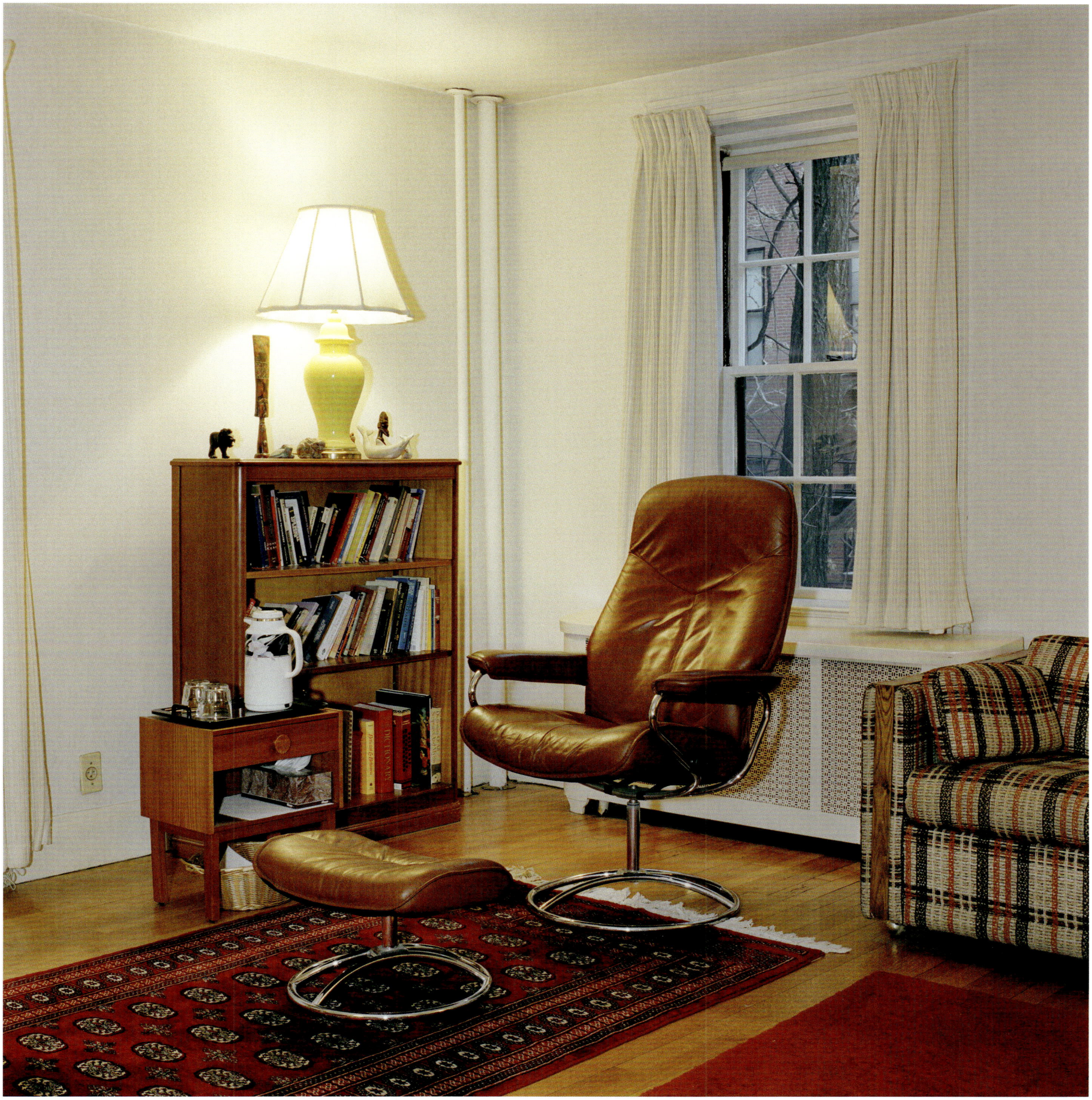
DICTIONARY

Cambridge, MA
Office with clay tile floor and blue analyst's chair, 2000

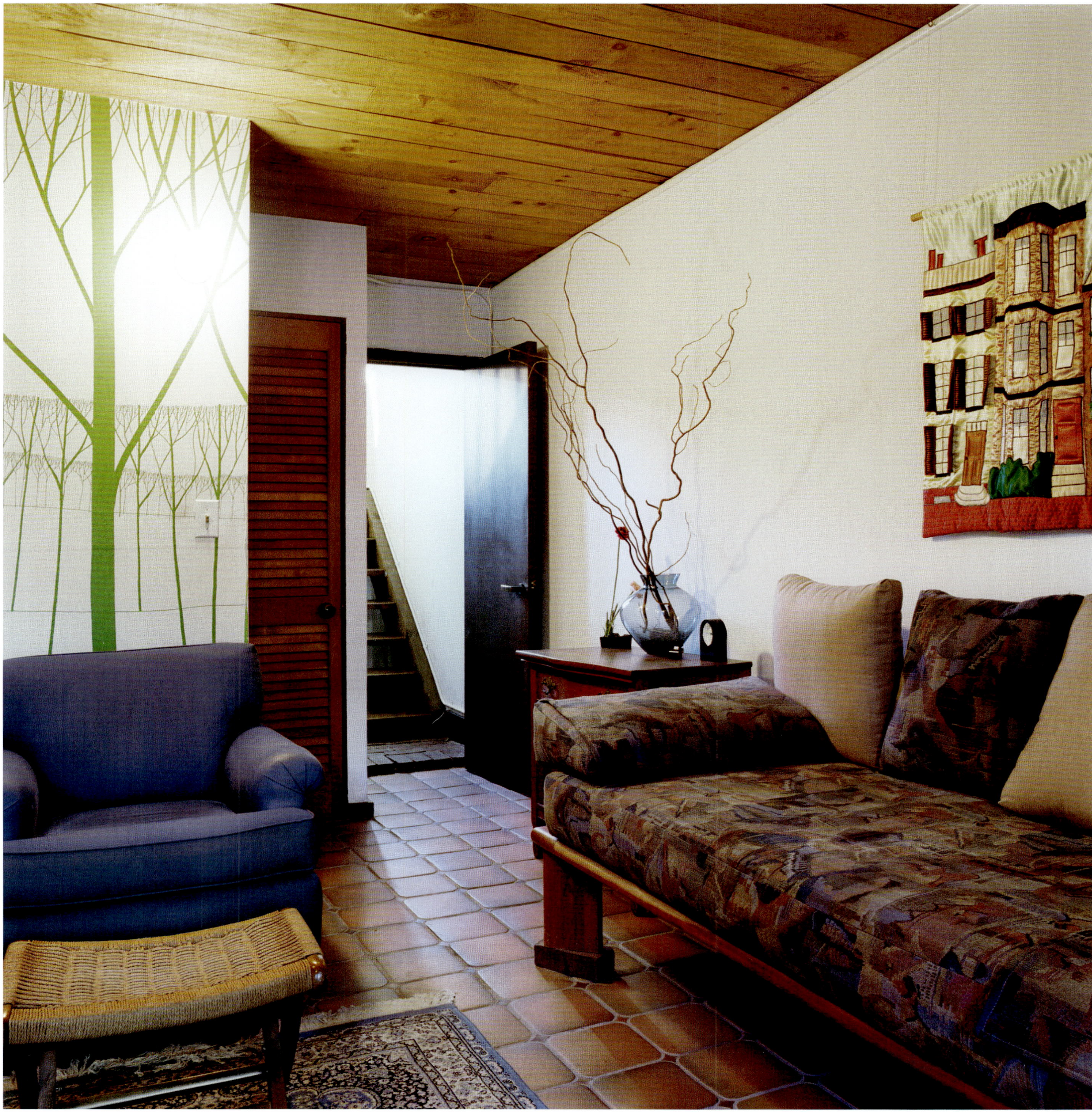

Buenos Aires
Office with gray shag rug and black leather chair and couch, 1999

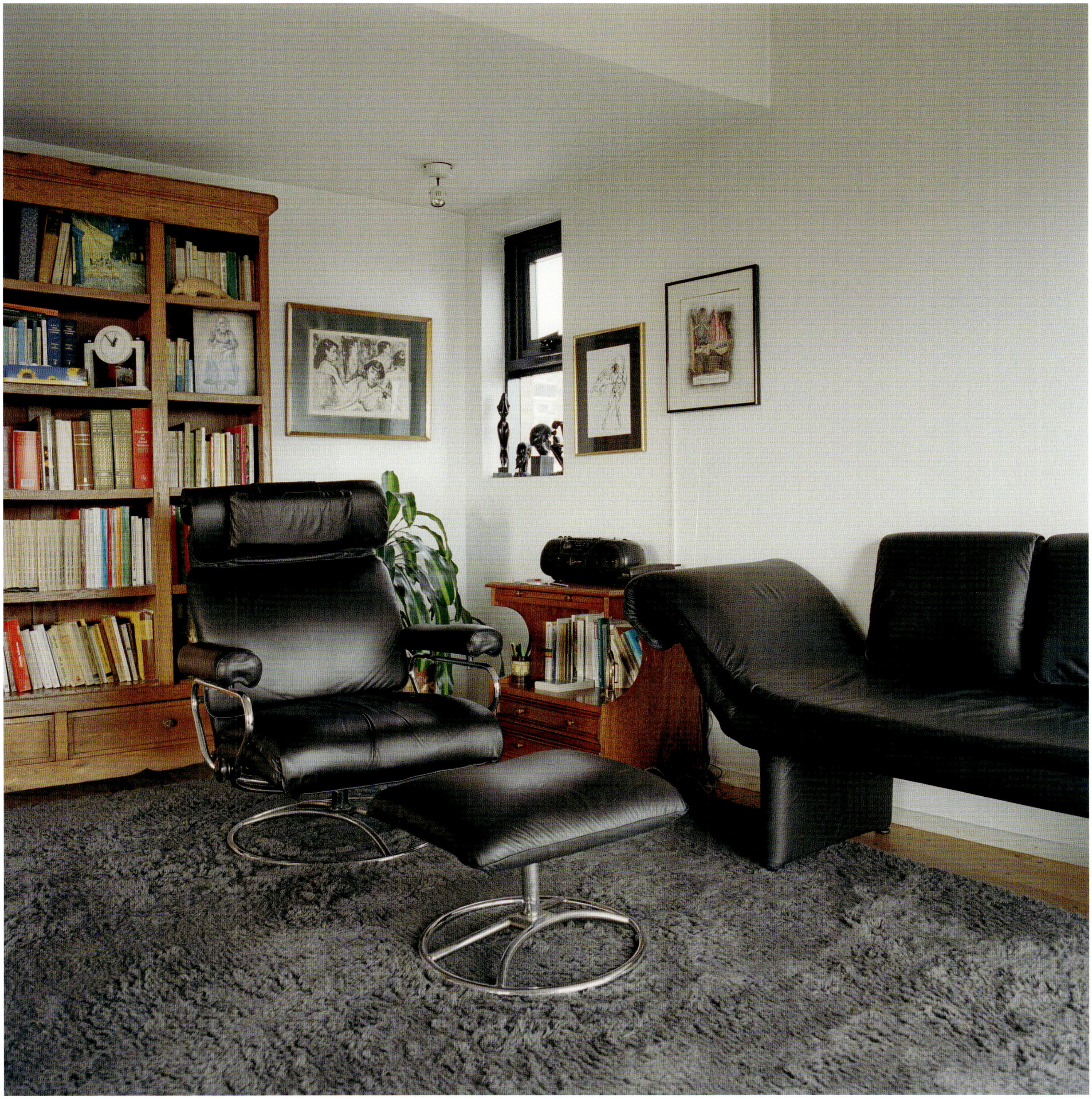

Belmont, MA
Attic office with red patient's chair and ship's clock, 2000

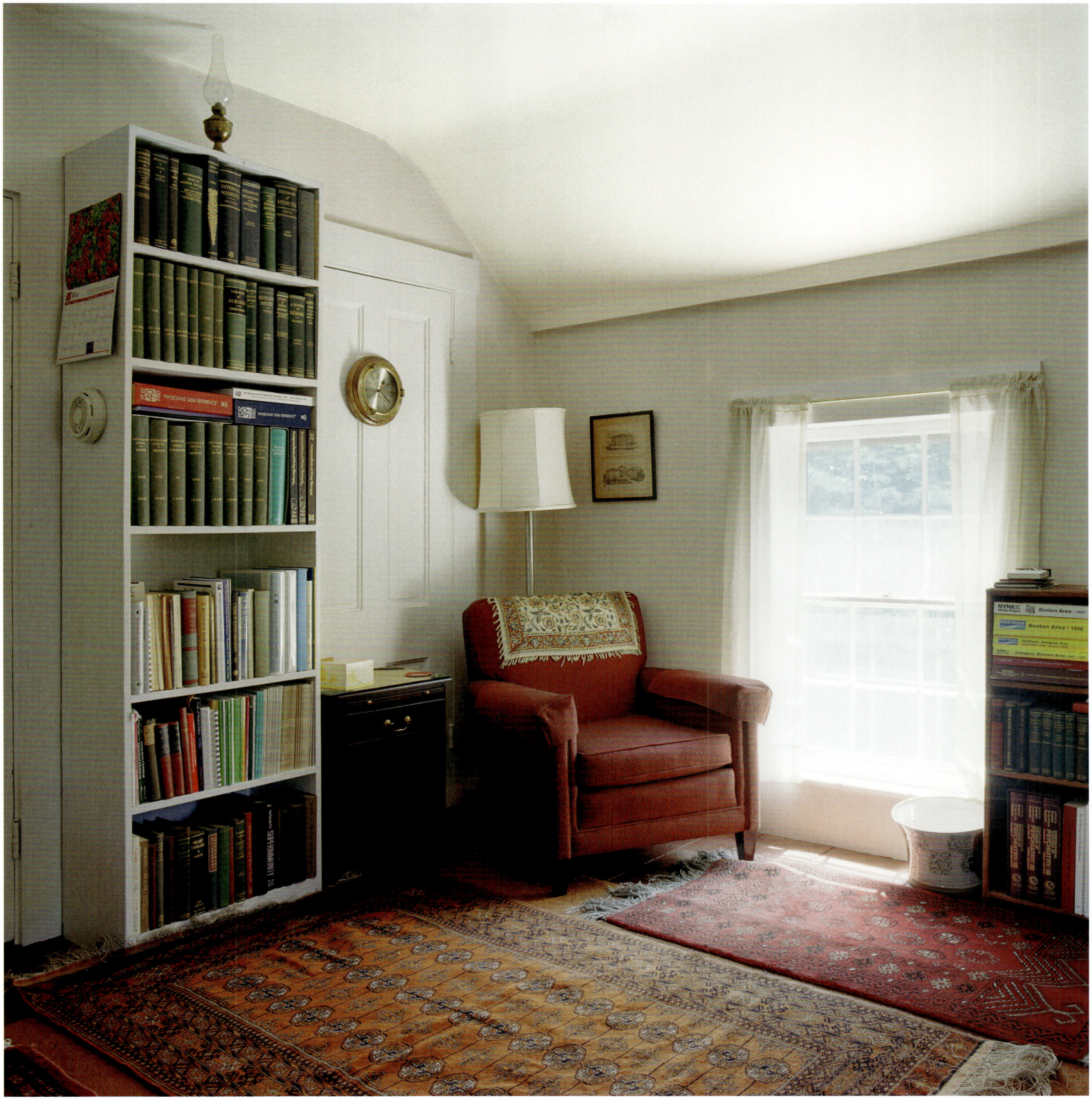

Belmont, MA
Analyst's chair with cat paintings and bookcase, 2000

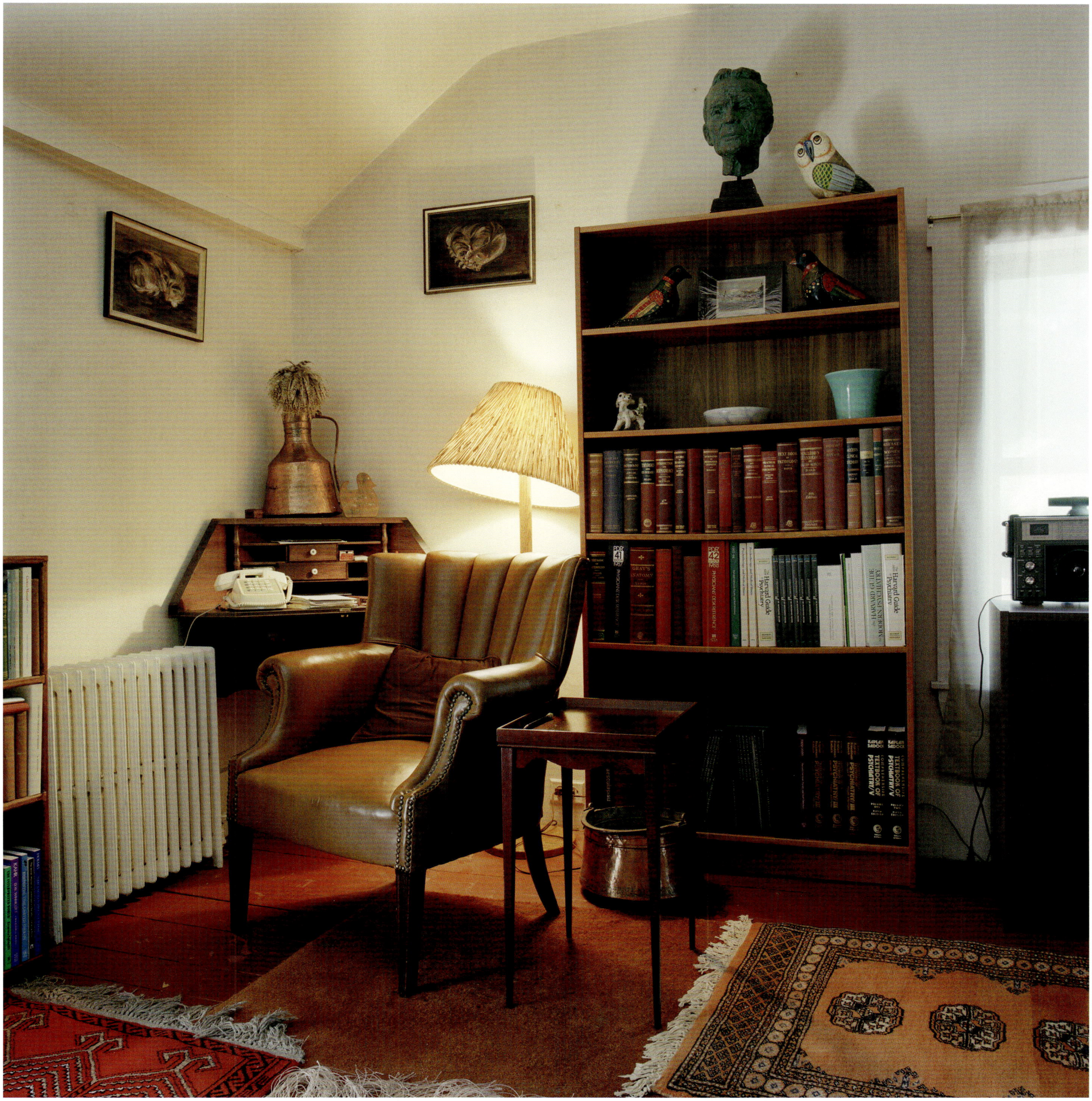

Lexington, MA
Office with polar bear sculptures and daffodil plant, 2000

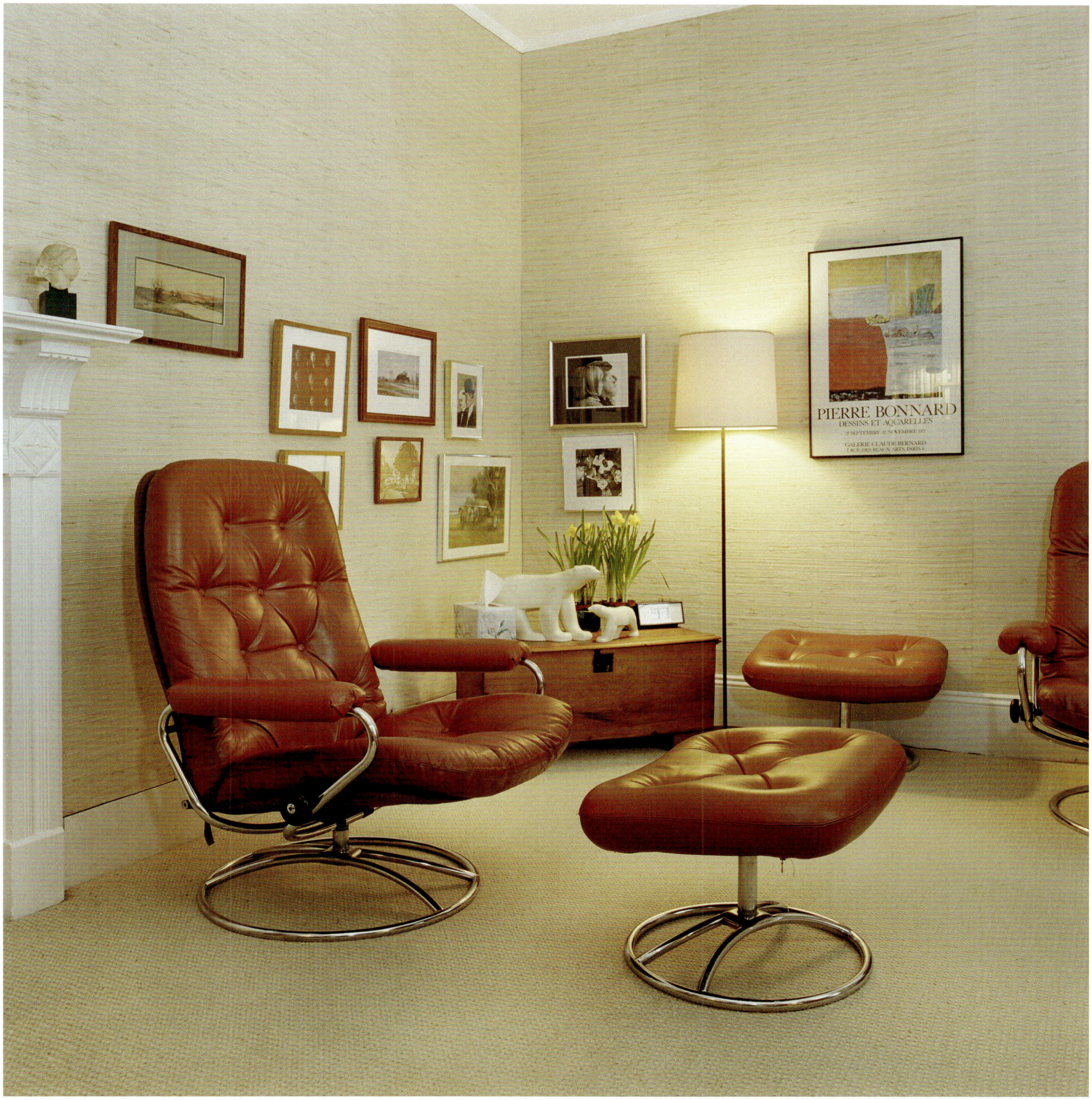
PIERRE BONNARD
DESSINS ET AQUARELLES
GALERIE CLAUDE BERNARD

Lexington, MA
Basement office with blue leather analyst's chair and carved wooden side table, 2000

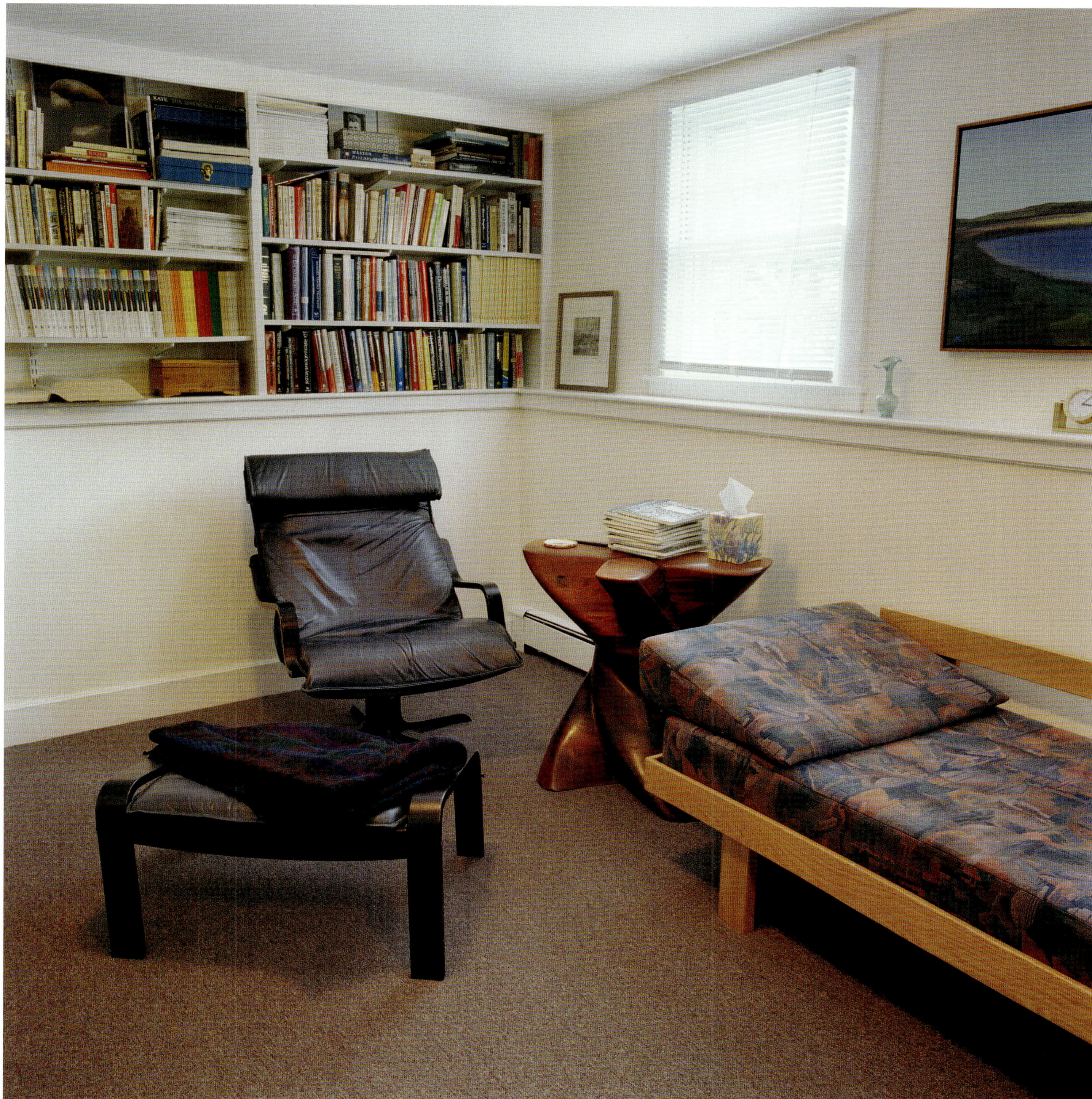

Auburndale, MA
Office with blue patterned antique couch and brown leather analyst's chair, 2000

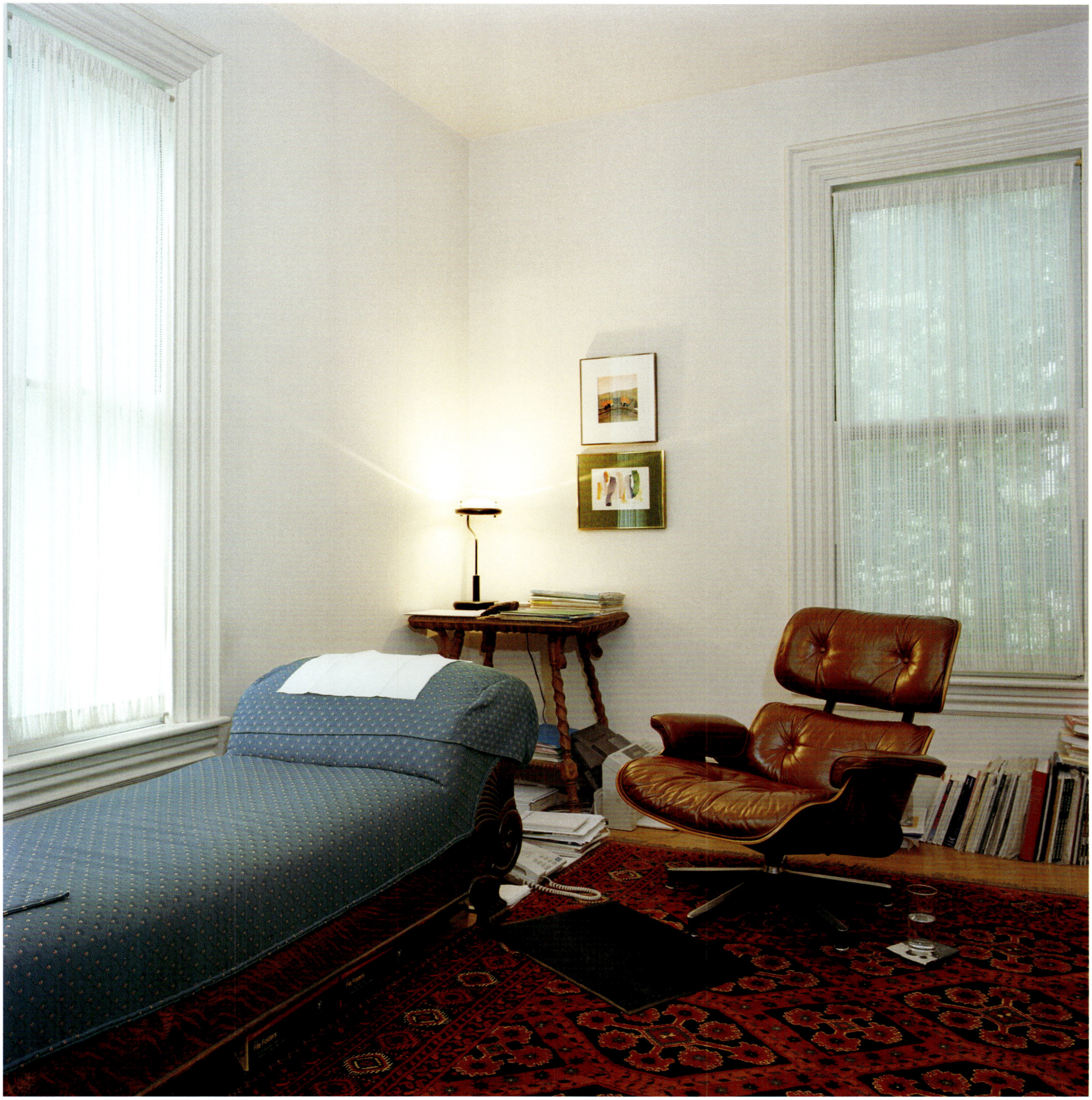

Stockbridge, MA
Office with soft beige leather couch and red striped pillow, 2000

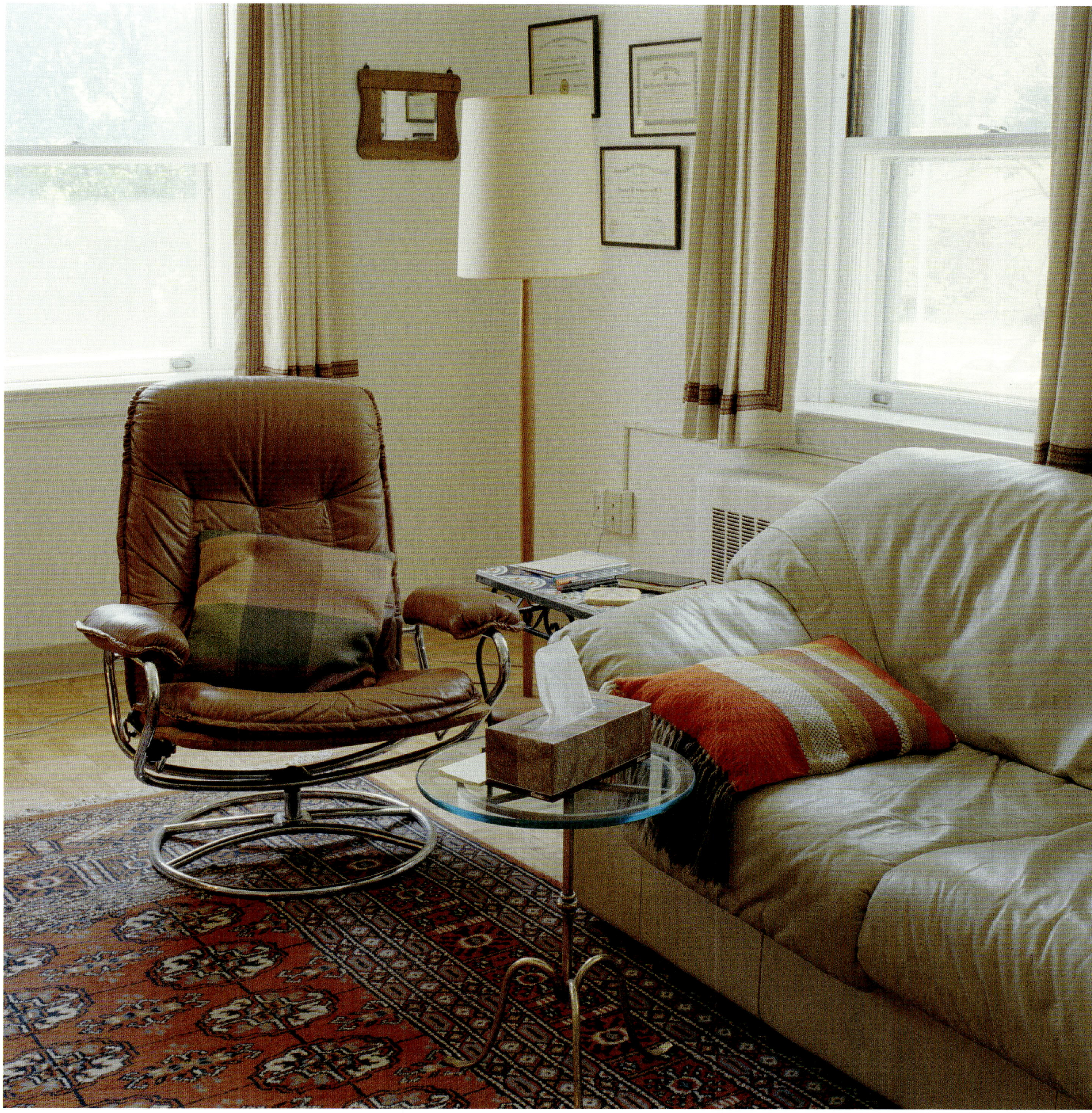

Waban, MA
Brown leather analyst's chair with two abstract paintings, 2000

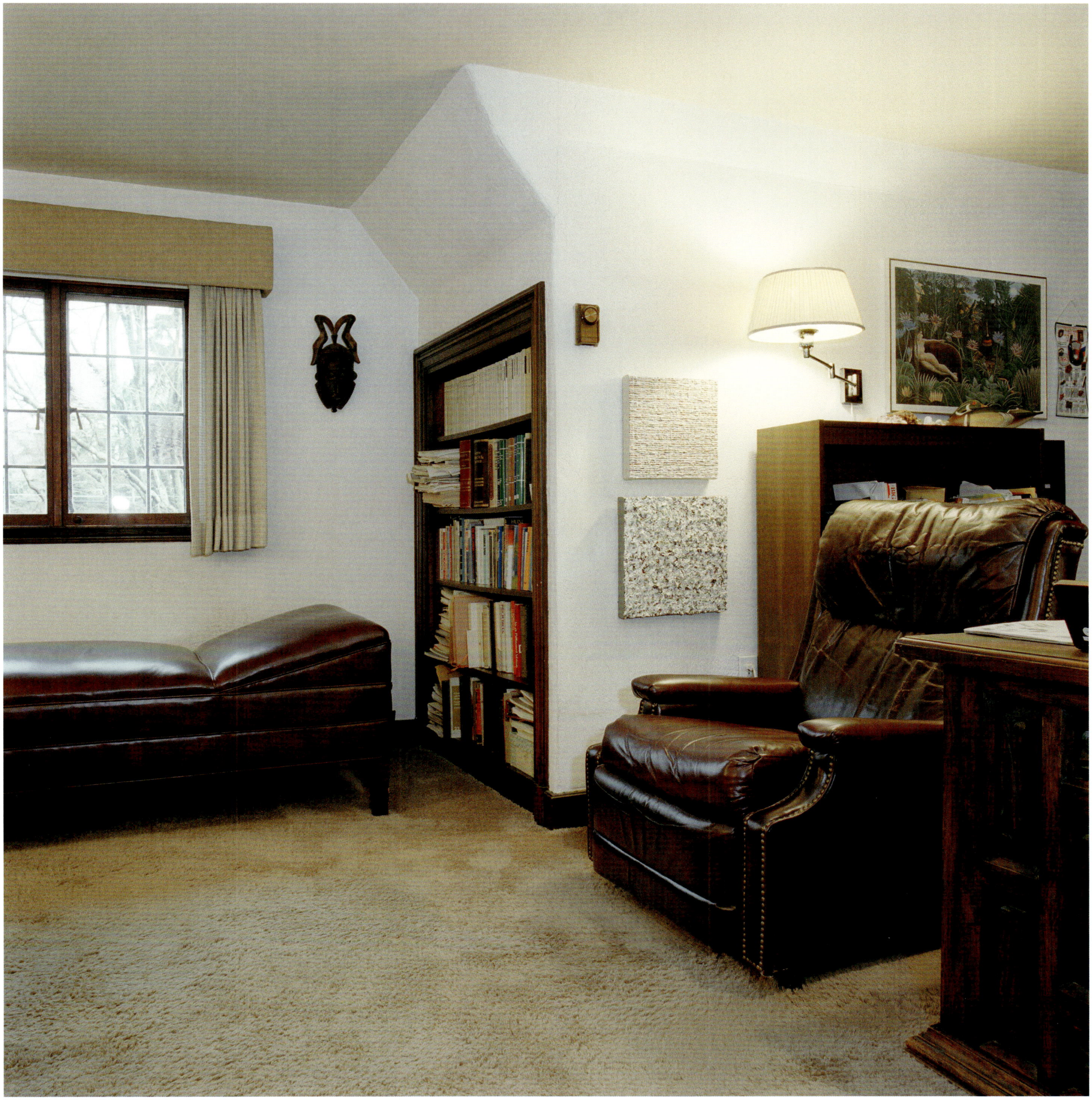

Cambridge, MA
Analyst's desk with bust of Freud and cloth cat, 2000

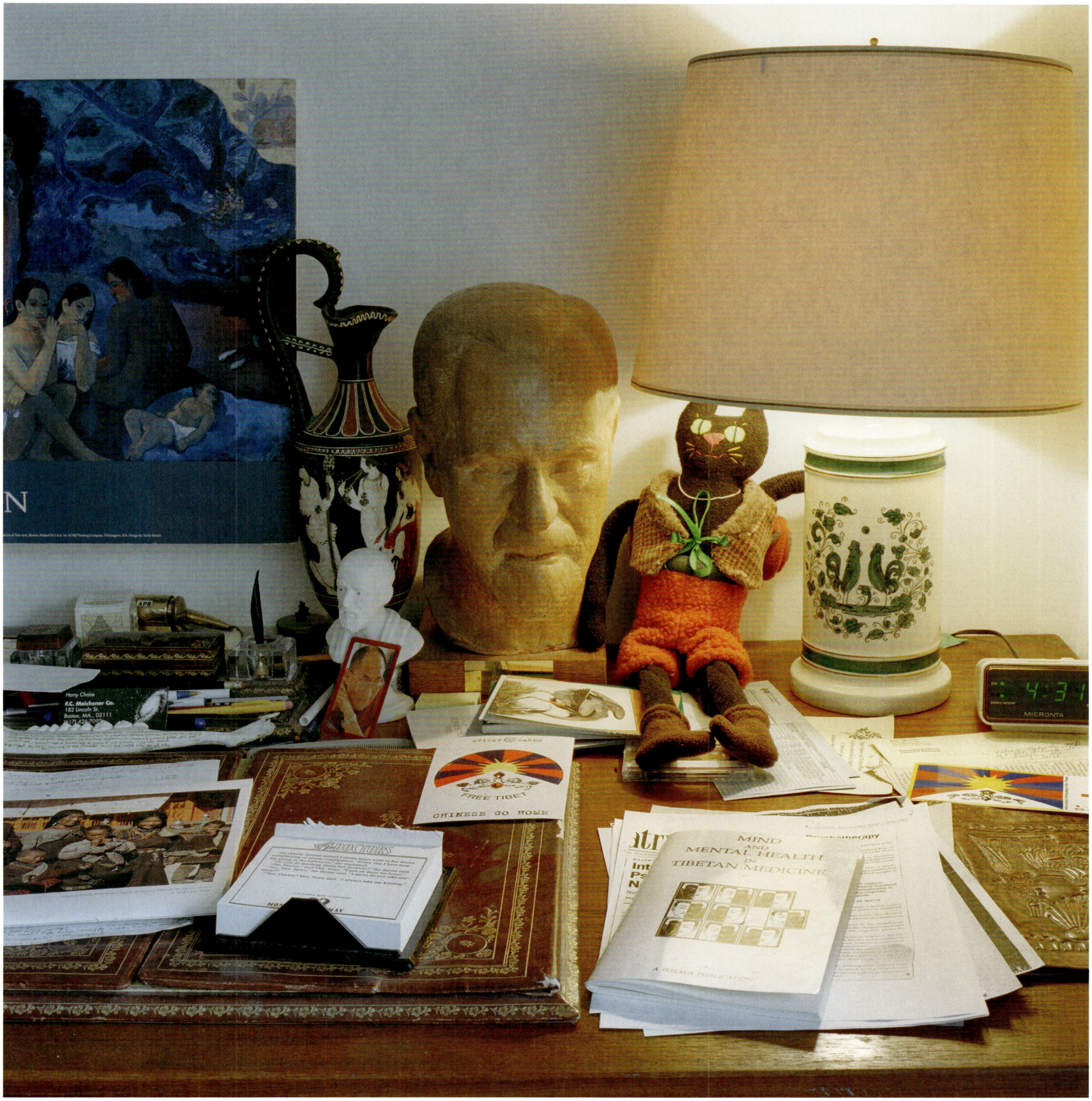
FREE TIBET
CHINESE GO HOME
MIND
AND
MENTAL HEALTH
IN
TIBETAN MEDICINE
MICRONTA

Newton, MA
Attic office with rug-covered couch, 2000

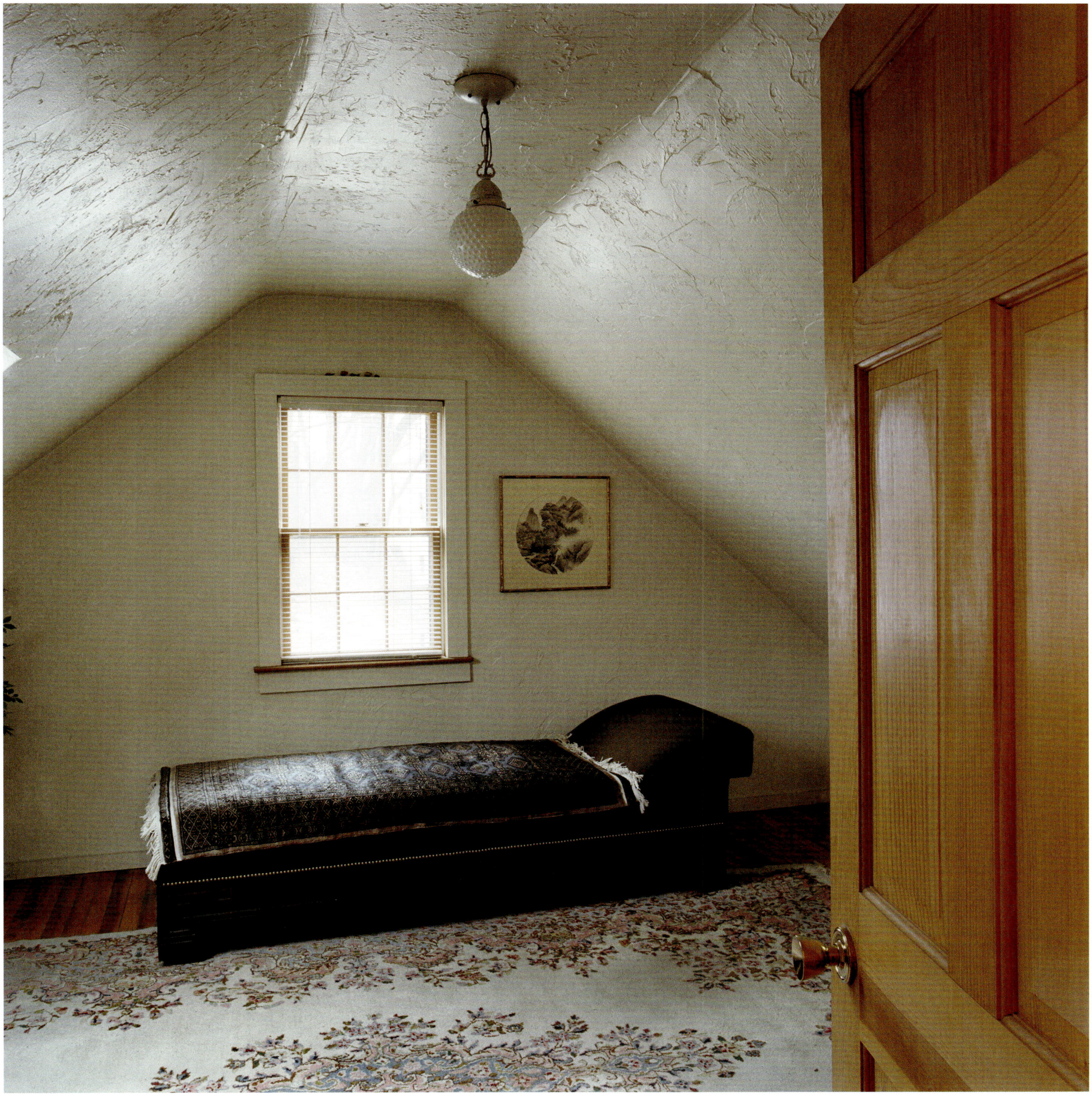

STARING INTO SPACE

Daniel Jacobs

The analytic office will forever be a space of paradox: a place of safety as well as danger. A place where one tries to hide from oneself among attempts at self-discovery. A place where it is a joy "to remain hidden and a disaster not to be found"[1]. It is a space that is at once private and shared; a space whose possession is contested. The objects in the rooms that Thurber captures incite shifting feelings of desire and distress as our associations drift among them. As Elizabeth A. Danze observes, "The room is [the analyst's] space, not mine. It has things in it and I look at [them] almost every day. After a while they start to become mine too, but not in the same way they are his. I don't know their history and I don't know his, but I start to overlay mine onto them."[2]

My own office offers me moments of comfort and melancholy alike. The ornate French commode belonged to my parents and to my childhood—both are gone now. The tanka above it was bought while on a trip to Nepal with my teenage son, who now has children of his own. The statue of a graceful Odissi dancer on the bookcase is a birthday gift from my wife. The African mask was a wedding present from an ill college friend, who had urged me to visit him soon. I didn't because of my own need to deny how little time he had left. He died the day before I arrived.

I am in constant visual contact with my history, my loves, my losses, my regrets, my joys. The plants in my office are not static. They grow and expand their lives. They have a future, if I care for them. The objects in my office help create an analytic attitude in me—one, I hope, that is open to tales of happiness and grief, of deferred dreams accompanied by plans for their final realization. And there is the light from three high windows—a light that is not steady, but changes within the hour and as the hours pass. In the shifting light of my consulting room and in the fresh flowers on the commode that will eventually fade, there are intimations of mortality.

My office is in my home, as are many in the Boston area. It reveals not only my aesthetic and clinical choices, but also the neighborhood in which I live and the class to which I belong. Upon arriving, patients walk along a pathway through a private garden that changes with each season. They notice how much or little attention has been given to it. Place and space are precipitants of memory, fear, and desire. Analytic offices tell us not only something of who the analysts are, but also how they wish to present themselves to their patients. Bookcases suggest a degree of scholarship. Clocks (sometimes visible to patients) emphasize time passing, their moving hands a concrete counterbalance to Freud's concept of the timeless unconscious.

Where analysts choose to place their chair and the measure of the distance behind, beside, or facing the subject, informs the patient how the analysis will proceed and what the analyst considers optimal for a psychoanalytic relationship. The analyst's ideas about proximity or distance may not match the patient's—a difference to be hopefully made explicit and explored in terms of memory, defense positions, and transferences on the part of both analyst and patient. In some of Thurber's images, the analytic chair seems to be placed at a distance from the couch as if to suggest that intimacy might not be easily achieved. In another, the analyst's chair seems out of proportion to the couch. Is there, in this arrangement, an unconscious message about the seat of authority?

I place my chair beside the psychoanalytic couch where my patients lie, close enough for them to be able to whisper if they wish, slightly behind, so as to see my patients fully prone and if need be, I can easily be seen by them with a turn of their head. I am hopeful that this positioning gives us each a certain amount of freedom to see or not see one another. Asking the patient to see the world horizontally is designed to change both the patient's and analyst's perspective, inner as well as outer. There are times when staring into space, rather than into a face, allows us room for the development of fantasy, memory or thought that the social interaction of vis-à-vis communication may limit.

That patients may or may not agree with my aesthetic choices and office arrangement is interesting to me. Their opinions often reveal aspects of transference. One woman found the overall shape of hundreds of small, seated Buddhist monks in my Nepalese tanka similar to an erect penis. She was upset that the image constantly faced her, while I remained out of sight. Some have felt embraced in the cocoon of my basement space with its high windows, while others have felt imprisoned by it. A supervisee, looking over the objects in my consulting room brought back from foreign places, thought of Indiana Jones—adventurer, explorer, plunderer. One patient felt my chair was too close, another, too far away.

I wonder about the covert messages conveyed to my patients by what I have chosen to place on my walls: a poster of Cristo's *Running Fence*, a photo of two Nepalese children, and another of a wooded trail. Am I saying with these pictures, "Let your mind run to childhood or to some path you have never trod"? And what of their messages to me in the gifts they bring—silk flowers in a glass case, homemade *baba au rhum*? Do these gifts express appreciation, or are they attempts to overcome anger or, perhaps, to display their talents? Do they say "remember me" or "take me in" or "continue to care"? The opportunity to explore the meaning behind these presents is the real gift.

All analytic offices are contemporary variations on a theme of desk, chair, couch, and the chosen objects which originally appeared in Freud's office in Vienna. In 1938, as the Freuds were preparing to flee Vienna for London, photographer Edmund Engelman was asked by August Aichhorn, a friend and colleague of Freud, to take photographs of Freud's office before it was too late. Ten days before the Freuds were scheduled to leave Vienna, Engelman arrived at Berggasse 19 with a small valise in which he hid his photographic equipment from the Gestapo. He took 150 photographs, using only natural light—a light that in black and white adds a sobriety and even menace to the rooms, perhaps capturing the terrible moment of our knowing, as Engelman did, that what we see will not last.

Engelman himself escaped Vienna a few months later without his negatives, only managing to retrieve them from Anna Freud after the war. Looking at these iconic photographs once more, I cannot help but feel I am being watched as I enter Freud's office, with its many small statues eyeing me from another time. But I also look around with fascination. On his wall, a marble frieze depicts Hector, that slain Trojan hero carried aloft by his comrades, while on the nearby desk Egyptian burial objects exist in perpetual mourning. It is a reminder of my own mortality and Freud's, of wars past and present, and of men's endless need to wage them. I can picture Rat Man or Wolf Man, Princess Bonaparte or Sándor Ferenczi entering this consulting room, lying on the carpeted couch, telling Freud their secrets (and keeping some to themselves). Engelman wrote of the office, "wherever one looked, there was a glimpse into the past."[3]

Unlike Engelman's 1938 images, Thurber's take advantage of color. The offices she portrays are brighter, often less cluttered. They are alive, ready for use—even hopeful. They reflect less of Freud's pessimism about the human race. The history of these offices, unlike Freud's, are unknown to us and therefore cast a lesser shadow. They hang suspended in the present. What are they waiting for, exactly? Perhaps for an answer as to how much psychoanalysis can help us. Thurber's images keep us in suspense, expecting, wondering, dreaming. They remind us where we live: between coming and going, living and dying, amidst what has happened to us and what is yet to come.

1 —— Donald Winnicott, *The Maturational Processes and the Facilitating Environment: Studies in the Theory of Emotional Development* (Madison: International Universities Press, 1965), 187.
2 —— Elizabeth A. Danze, "An Architect's View of Introspective Space. The Analytic Vessel," *The Annual of Psychoanalysis*, 33 (2005): 109.
3 —— Edmund Engelman. *Berggasse 19: Sigmund Freud's Home and Offices, Vienna 1938*. New York; Basic Books, 1976.

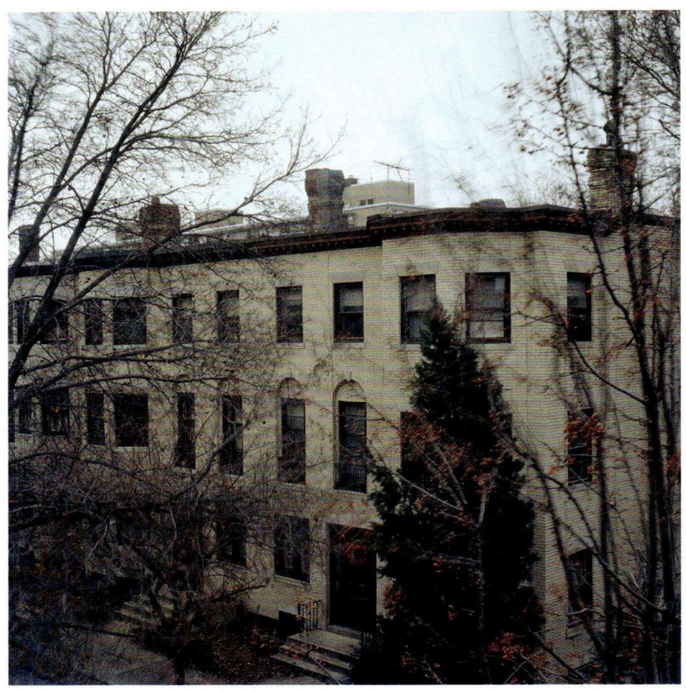

ACKNOWLEDGEMENTS

I am fortunate to have many friends and family members who have encouraged and believed in me over the course of my life. My thanks go out to all of them. There are a few that I would like to specifically thank for their support of this work.

The genesis of this project was a photography trip that I took to Buenos Aires with Jim Dow in 1999. I want to thank both Jim and Jacquie Dow for suggesting that I tag along and for their friendship and support over the years.

I would also like to thank Dr. Gela Rosenthal, a psychoanalyst in Buenos Aires who, when I asked to photograph her office, immediately contacted several of her friends who in turn opened up their offices to me. This work wouldn't have happened without her.

I want to extend my sincere thanks to all the analysts who contributed to this project in a variety of ways. Their generosity of time and spirit in making themselves and their offices available to me was deeply appreciated. I would like to thank both Dr. William Ackerly and Dr. Lora Tessman in particular for their many kindnesses and friendship.

Dr. Dan Jacobs was especially instrumental in helping me get this project off the ground in Boston. From the beginning he championed me and became a good friend. I suspect he probably talked a few reluctant colleagues into participating. I am grateful to him for all his help and for the beautiful essay he wrote for the book.

Through their tireless advocacy and friendship, Lia Gangitano, Milena Kalinovska and Stephen Hepworth have been pivotal players in my journey as an artist. I would like to thank them all, especially Lia for her wonderful introduction.

I would also like to thank Jess T. Dugan for all their encouragement and help over the years. I am deeply grateful for their friendship and for their insightful and sensitive approach to the interview.

I have been fortunate to have the support of the Krakow Witkin Gallery in Boston. I would like to thank Barbara Krakow, Andrew Witkin, Ryan Cross and Skyela Heitz for all their work on my behalf.

The Bunting Fellowship that I received in 2000 allowed me the financial and institutional support needed to pursue this project. I would like to thank the Radcliffe Institute for Advanced Study at Harvard University as well as Judith Batalion who was my stellar research assistant and contributed to the project in myriad ways.

I would also like to thank Susan Unterberg and Gaby Collins-Fernandez of the Anonymous Was a Woman foundation for their early support.

My deepest thanks to Klaus Kehrer for taking this project on and to the entire team at Kehrer Verlag who have made this process such a pleasure. I would especially like to thank Benjamin Wolbergs, Aydria Stadter, Erik Clewe, Patrick Horn and Nicole Fong. I would also like to thank Kent Rodzwicz who contributed his many skills and impeccable eye to the production of the book here in Boston and Andrea Volpe for her help with the editing.

And last but certainly not least, I would like to express my gratitude to Dr. B. This project was inspired by the work that we did over many years and it is my profound regret that he never lived to see the book that he relentlessly but gently pushed me to make. *Analysis* is also dedicated to him.

AUTHORS

Lia Gangitano
is the founder and director of Participant Inc. in New York City.

Jess T. Dugan
is an artist whose work explores issues of identity through photography, video, and writing.

Daniel Jacobs
is a Training and Supervising Analyst at the Boston Psychoanalytic Society and Institute and Director of the Hanns Sachs Library and Archives there. He is also Director of the Center for Advanced Psychoanalytic Studies in Princeton.

Project Management: Kehrer Verlag (Aydria Stadter)
Texts: Jess T. Dugan, Lia Gangitano, Daniel Jacobs, Shellburne Thurber
Copy Editing: Nicole R. Fong
Design: Kehrer Design (Benjamin Wolbergs)
Image Processing: Kehrer Design (Erik Clewe, Patrick Horn)
Production Management: Kehrer Design (Tom Streicher)

Image on p. 2
Cambridge, MA
Office with blue fabric couch and three wall prints, 2000

Bibliographic information published by the Deutsche Nationalbibliothek
The Deutsche Nationalbibliothek lists this publication in the Deutsche Nationalbibliografie; detailed bibliographic data is available on the Internet at http://dnb.dnb.de.

Printed and bound in Germany

ISBN 978-3-96900-096-0

Kehrer Verlag Heidelberg
www.kehrerverlag.com